My Garden Book
This book belongs to
Seeds
My Garden Book
My Garden Book
My Garden Book

Contents

Hello & Welcome, Adults!

Dear parents and carers,

My First Gardening Book has been designed as a tool to empower your youngsters in growing their own food. Even though it is your child's book, your role in this adventure is vital as supporters, guiding and supervising your child in practical tasks like filling pots with compost, planting seeds, caring for the seedlings, as well as measuring, reading, writing and recording. While your child takes charge of growing food, your involvement "cultivates" their essential life skills and helps them develop a strong connection with themselves and the natural world around them.

Regardless of how much physical space you have available for growing food (a window sill or a big garden), ***My First Gardening Book*** has been created to serve as a guide for shared moments of learning, inspiring curiosity, teaching responsibility, instilling patience, nurturing perseverance and promoting an overall growth in your child.

This book will help you embark on a practical gardening journey together; your support will enhance experiences and facilitate both plant growth and child character building.

Welcome to ***My First Gardening Book*** where the rewards abound for everyone involved!

Chapter 1 - The Adventure Begins
The adventure begins
The adventure begins
The adventure begins
The adventure begins
?!
?!

The Garden Adventure Begins

The new house had a shed at the back of the garden.

Sam and Mia pulled open the creaky door and looked inside. Rusty tools and an old hose were hanging on the walls; a dusty gardening book lay open on the small shelf.

"Oh, it says here that carrots grow in the ground!" Sam's eyes widened as he examined the book.

"No way!
Do they really come from the dirt?"
Mia was amazed too.

For dinner that evening, the family had roasted vegetables.

"Mum, Dad, did you know that carrots grow in the mud?" the twins were very excited to share.

"Yeah, they start from tiny little seeds!" Sam added eagerly.

Mum smiled.

"My grandad used to grow tomatoes and runner beans. I remember they were very tasty!" Mum said.

Dad replied, "My grandma grew the juiciest strawberries!"

The family started talking about growing their own fruit and vegetables.

Then the parents had an idea!

Mr Parker from next door grows potatoes in his garden. He may be willing to teach you what to do.

The twins' eyes sparkled. The next day, Sam and Mia started learning about the vegetables they enjoyed eating.

Mum and Dad were very helpful. They bought the twins "My First Gardening Book", just like the book you are reading now!

In their new book, Sam and Mia could keep track of their discoveries, write about their plants and draw pictures. This is how Sam and Mia's gardening adventure began.

Sam, we can grow our plants in pots and in grow bags!

What plants shall we start with, Mia?

The plants we suggest in this book are not only easy to grow but also fascinating to watch as well as tasty to eat.

1. Potatoes are versatile and easy to grow in containers or grow bags. Your child will love uncovering them from the soil.

2. Cherry tomatoes are a great choice, especially if your garden space is limited. Some bushy varieties can grow in hanging baskets and pots. They are prolific croppers which means you'll have a steady supply of tasty cherry tomatoes.

3. Strawberries are children's favourites. Children love eating the fruit and watching the berries ripen.

4. Carrots are a snack that children love eating. They grow best in compost and deep pots.

5. Lettuces are easy to grow so they make a great choice for first-time gardeners, and you will enjoy fresh home-grown salad leaves.

6. Beetroot are not fussy at all and tolerate shade.

7. Peas are climbers so they need support and grow well in pots, in a sunny spot.

8. Runner beans are very tall climbers (need support) but they are easy to take care of and can add some extra excitement to the garden. Use a heavy pot that will not tip with the weight of the plant.

9. Cucumbers love warmth so start them early on in the season but keep them indoors until the danger of frost has passed. Choose a bushy variety if you are short of space and keep the soil moist.

10. Pumpkins! Why not grow your own Halloween lantern? This experience will teach your child to treat food with respect, and we suggest you cook the pumpkin after it's done its "lantern" job.

It's essential to select plants based on your available space. A spacious garden can accommodate a variety, while a more confined window sill, balcony or patio may only have room for a select few. Guide your child in choosing the most suitable plants.

Chapter 3 provides simple instructions on planting/sowing/caring for each of the 10 plants suggested above. Also note the extra "Tips for Parents" featured for each of them. You may need to help your child read and follow the instructions for best results.

Chapter 2 - Getting ready

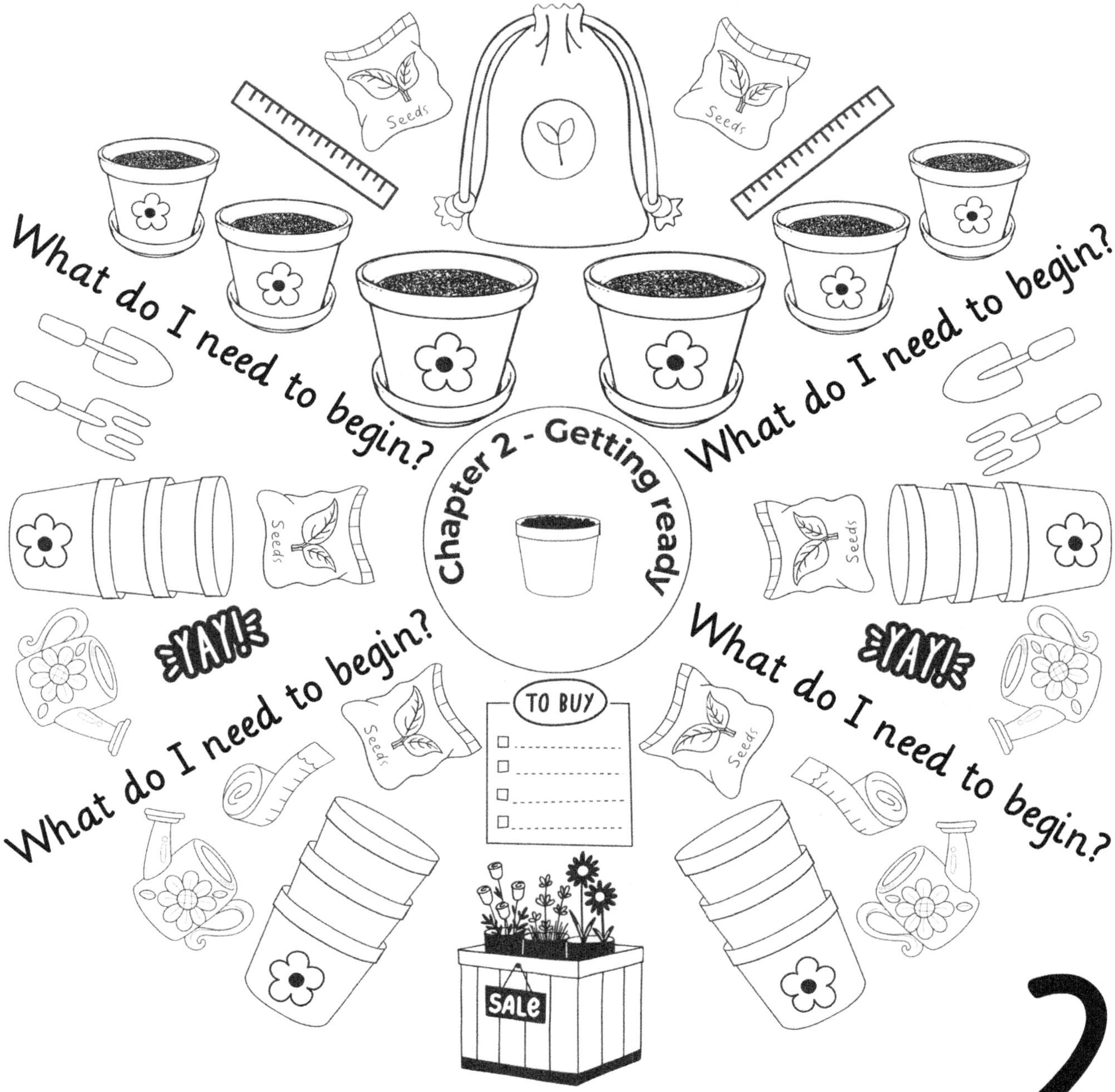

2

What do I need to begin?

Mr Parker, the next door neighbour, worked in the local garden centre. He had an allotment too.

"Let's visit Mr Parker. He'll show you what plants you can grow in pots. Grab your Gardening Book and let's go!" said Mum, and the family drove to the garden centre.

Mr Parker was very helpful. He started by explaining about compost, "Compost is your plant's food. If you give your plants good food, they will be healthy!"

The twins had never heard of compost before. It was fascinating!

Mr Parker showed the family around and answered their questions. The twins made a list of 10 plants they could grow in pots at home.

1. Potatoes - in deep pots or grow bags.
2. Cherry tomatoes - in grow bags or big pots.
3. Strawberries - a big pot.
4. Carrots - a deep pot
5. Lettuces are easy to grow.
6. Beetroot are not fussy.
7. Peas climb. We must buy sticks or a net.
8. Runner beans climb even higher than peas!
9. Cucumbers will also need sticks or a net.
10. We can grow our own pumpkin for Halloween!

Back home, Sam and Mia started planning their garden. They made a shopping list too.

What plant do I want to grow?

Where shall I grow it?

- ☐ a pot
- ☐ a grow bag
- ☐ in the ground

What plant do I want to grow?

Where shall I grow it?

- ☐ a pot
- ☐ a grow bag
- ☐ in the ground

What plant do I want to grow?

Where shall I grow it?

- ☐ a pot
- ☐ a grow bag
- ☐ in the ground

What plant do I want to grow?

Where shall I grow it?

- ☐ a pot
- ☐ a grow bag
- ☐ in the ground

What plant do I want to grow?

Where shall I grow it?

- ☐ a pot
- ☐ a grow bag
- ☐ in the ground

What plant do I want to grow?

Where shall I grow it?

- ☐ a pot
- ☐ a grow bag
- ☐ in the ground

What plant do I want to grow?

Where shall I grow it?

- ☐ a pot
- ☐ a grow bag
- ☐ in the ground

What plant do I want to grow?

Where shall I grow it?

- ☐ a pot
- ☐ a grow bag
- ☐ in the ground

What plant do I want to grow?

Where shall I grow it?

- ☐ a pot
- ☐ a grow bag
- ☐ in the ground

What plant do I want to grow?

Where shall I grow it?

- ☐ a pot
- ☐ a grow bag
- ☐ in the ground

What plant do I want to grow?

Where shall I grow it?

- ☐ a pot
- ☐ a grow bag
- ☐ in the ground

What plant do I want to grow?

Where shall I grow it?

- ☐ a pot
- ☐ a grow bag
- ☐ in the ground

My Garden Plan

My Garden Plan

My Shopping List

Plants, Seeds:	Compost, Pots, Tools I need:
☐	☐ compost
☐	☐ trowel or a little spade
☐	☐ watering can
☐	☐
☐	☐
☐	☐
☐	☐
☐	☐
☐	☐
☐	☐

My Shopping List

Plants, Seeds:	Other Things:
☐	☐
☐	☐
☐	☐
☐	☐
☐	☐
☐	☐
☐	☐
☐	☐
☐	☐
☐	☐

TIPS FOR GROWN-UPS

If you are new to gardening, don't worry because chapter 3 provides simple instructions on planting/sowing/caring for each of the 10 plants suggested in this book.

Additionally, each plant features extra "Tips for Parents" that we hope will be helpful for you as a gardening mentor.

Help your child to read and follow the instructions carefully for best results.

If you have further questions, there is help in our friendly Garden Growers Community which you can join for free by scanning the QR code below:

Chapter 3 - Planting
Let's start planting
Let's start planting
Let's start planting
Let's start planting
Let's start planting
Let's start planting

3

Mr Parker's Planting Lesson

Mr Parker is here, kiddos!
He's got something for you.

Sam and Mia dashed to greet Mr Parker.

Mr Parker handed Sam
an egg box with chitted potatoes.

"Now we need compost!" he smiled
and gave Mia two of the grow bags.

Out in the garden, they placed the grow bags in the sun.

The twins put some compost at the bottom of their grow bags just like Mr Parker demonstrated. Then it was time for the egg box.

"Why are these potatoes in an egg box, Mr Parker?" Mia was very curious.

"To keep their chit safe, Mia. Can you see the shoots? I put these potatoes on the window sill 4 weeks ago and now they are ready to plant," explained Mr Parker.

He carefully placed two potatoes on the compost, chit facing up.

The twins did the same.

Then they covered the potatoes with compost but didn't fill the bags to the top.

"In a couple of weeks time, when leaves pop out, you will add more compost, just enough to cover them. As they keep growing, you keep burying them until you fill up the whole bag. " Mr Parker explained.

Finally, Mr Parker showed the twins how to water the potato bags. Sam and Mia had their first garden crop planted.

Everyone was happy: it was time for a delicious cup of tea.

The heaviest potato ever grown weighed 4.98kg, which is almost as heavy as a small dog!
The tallest potato plant ever was 2.85m! This is just about as tall as a basketball hoop!
Tuber
Tuber
We are not roots; we are actually the swollen parts of underground stems called tubers.
Tuber
We came from South America. We can be red, purple and even blue!
Tuber

How to Grow Potatoes

Early potatoes grow faster.

1. Place the potatoes on a window sill for 4-6 weeks or until 1-2cm shoots appear.

2. Fill a third of the grow bag with compost and put it in a sunny spot.

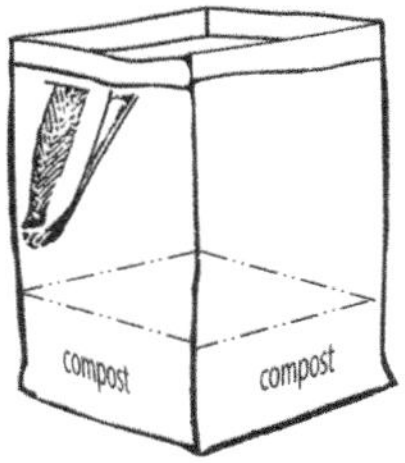

3. Place 2 chitted potatoes on top of the compost.

4. Cover the potatoes carefully with the same amount of compost. Don't fill the whole bag.

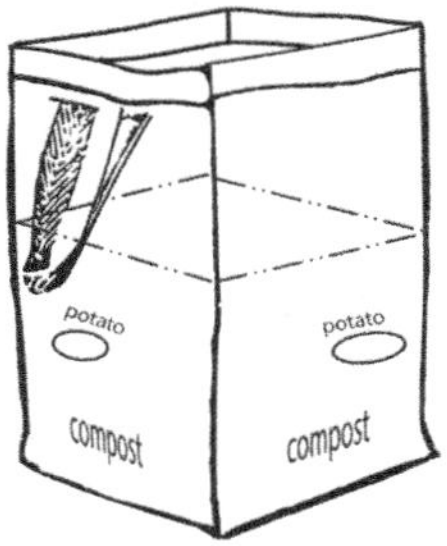

5. Water well until the soil appears soaked through.

6. Water the plants regularly.

7. When potato leaves come out, add just enough compost to bury them. Repeat this until you fill up the bag.

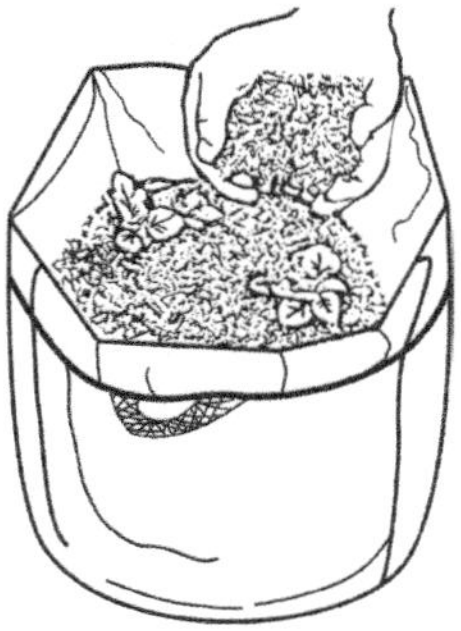

8. The plants will produce flowers. The potatoes are ready to harvest when the flowers start to die off.

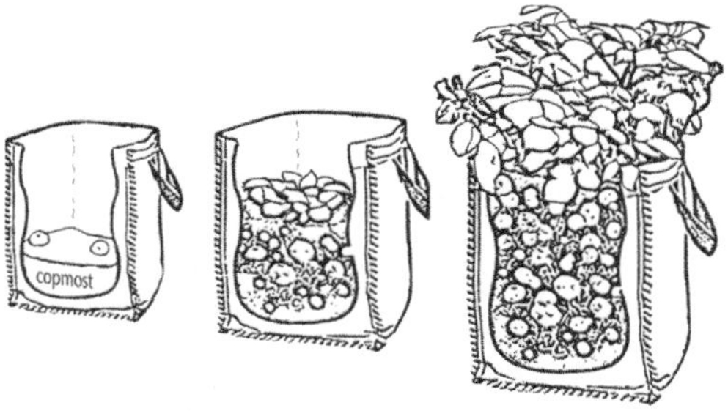

Tips for Parents:

Help your child select a sunny location. Help them to lift heavy grow bags, pots. Encourage your child to observe the plants as they grow and water then regularly.

Once a plant grew 1,269 cherry tomatoes! Can you count that far?
In a town called Buñol in Spain, they have a huge tomato fight festival. People throw tomatoes at each other. It's messy but great fun!
The *heaviest* tomato weighed 5.28kg and it measured 82.5cm around!
Cherry tomatoes are generally much sweeter than large tomatoes. They come in lots of different colours and sizes!

How to Grow Cherry Tomatoes

Make it easy. Pick young tomato plants from the garden centre.

1. The bigger the pot for your tomato plant, the better. Place it in the sunniest spot and put some compost in it.

2. Water the tomato plant in its original small pot before gently taking it out. Squeeze the pot to loosen the roots up if the plant doesn't want to come out.

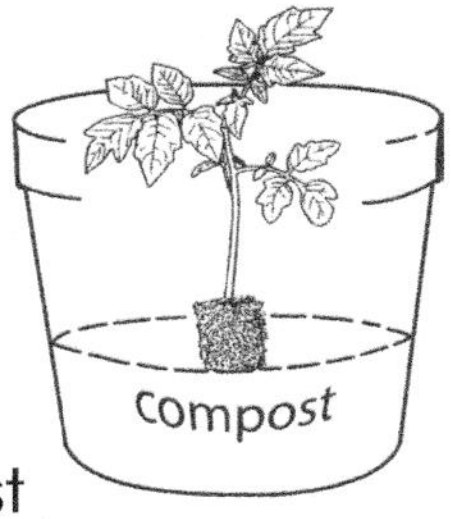

3. Place the plant on the compost and start adding compost around it. Bury the roots and stem all the way up to the first set of leaves.

4. Press down on the compost to firm it around the plant and water the pot well.

5. Some cherry tomatoes need a strong cane (a long stick) for support. As the main stem grows, tie it to the cane with a thick string.

6. Keep the soil evenly moist.

Tips for Parents:

Together choose the tomato plants from the garden centre. Go for bushy varieties if you are short on space. Discuss the planting process and help with tying the stem to the cane. Remind your child to water the plants regularly.

Strawberries *aren't true* berries because they have their seeds on the outside.

The *heaviest* strawberry weighed 322g. This is as heavy as a can of coke!

Strawberries contain more *vitamin* C than oranges!
They come in different sizes and flavours.
Some strawberries are really small.

How to Grow Strawberries

If planting more than one strawberry plant in the same pot, space them 20-30cm apart. You will need a big pot for that.

1. Fill the pot with compost.

2. Water the young strawberry plant in its original pot before gently taking it out.

3. Dig a hole in the compost about the size of the plant's roots.

4. Place the plant in the hole and cover the roots with compost.

5. Make sure that the crown of the plant (the centre) is not covered with compost and it doesn't stick out too much.

6. Firmly pat down the soil around the plant and water well.

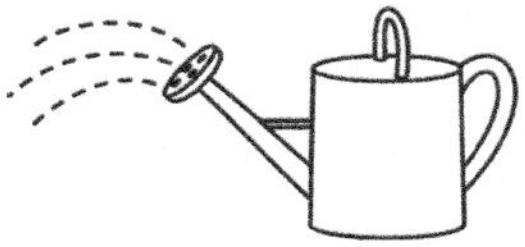

7. Strawberries need regular watering, especially in hot and sunny weather.

Tips for Parents:

Help your child choose healthy plants from the garden centre. Help them plant at the right depth - not too deep, not too shallow. Remind them to water and teach them to avoid wetting the crown (centre) of the plant.

Carrot seeds are so *tiny* that one teaspoon can hold about 2000 carrot seeds.

Carrots come in more colours than just orange. You can find them in purple, red, yellow and white!

bounce!
bounce!
I'm strong!

The *longest* carrot was 6.25m long. That's about half a double-decker bus!

The *heaviest* carrot ever grown weighed an amazing 10.17kg, which is as heavy as two cats!

How to Grow Carrots

Choose a deep pot with holes at the bottom to let the water out.

1. Fill the pot with compost to the top and water it.

2. With your finger, make holes in the soil, about 2-3cm deep and 5-7cm apart. Carrots need space to grow healthy.

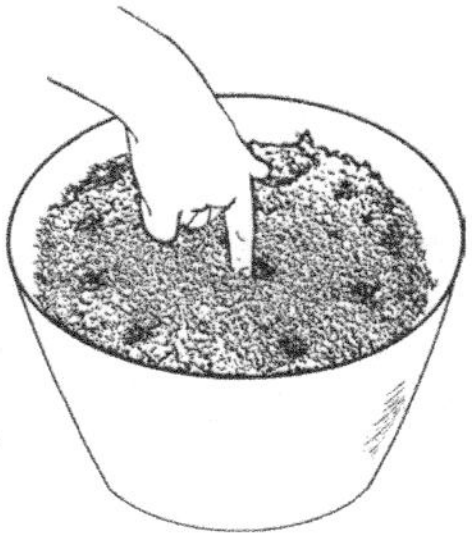

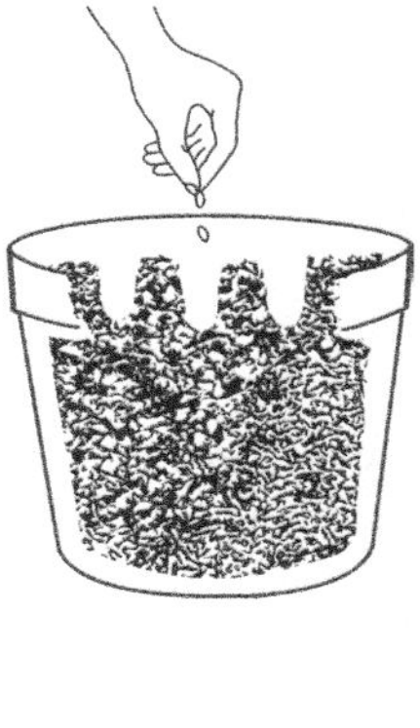

3. Drop two carrot seeds in each hole and cover with compost.

4. Water your carrots regularly. Do it more often in dry or warm periods. Keep the soil damp but not soggy.

5. Be patient. Carrots take 12-16 weeks to grow.

If you start early in the year, you can do this twice!

Tips for Parents:

For carrots, the deeper the pot, the better. Help your child choose a pot that is at least 30 cm deep. Encourage your child to check the soil moisture regularly and water if needed. Show your child how to identify the weeds and pull them out.

The fastest someone has ever eaten a whole head of lettuce was in just 47sec! It wasn't a snail...
We, Lettuces, are cousins with Sunflowers!
?
The ancient Egyptians were the first to grow lettuce as a food crop, 6000 years ago. This was a long time ago!
Lettuce come in shades of green, red and purple. The darker the leaves, the more nutritious they are.
ANCIENT EGYPT
!

How to Grow Lettuce

1. Fill up a pot with compost and firm it down a little.

2. Scatter some lettuce seeds thinly on the surface.

   Aim for about 1-2cm between the seeds so they have space to grow.

3. Cover them with a thin layer of compost and water them gently.

4. Keep your lettuces well watered.

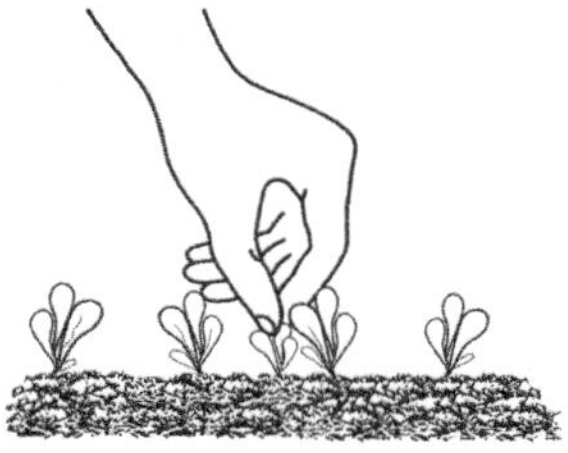

5. When the seedlings are about 2cm tall, pull the smaller ones out to give the rest space to grow.

6. Count 21 days and you can start picking the leaves that are big enough to eat.

21 Days Count

1 2 3 4 5 6 7

8 9 10 11 12 13 14

15 16 17 18 19 20 21

7. Pick leaves from around the outside of your plants.
   Pick them regularly and your plants will produce more yummy leaves!

Tips for Parents:

Lettuces prefer partial shade. Help your child with the sowing - seeds are small. Remind your child to water regularly and show them how to harvest the outside leaves that are ready. If the lettuces get "stressed", they'll start growing upwards to produce seed and the leaves turn bitter.

Beetroot juice makes strawberry jam and ice cream look better.
The *heaviest* beetroot ever was 24kg! This is as heavy as a child!
We like the colder, milder weather of spring and autumn, when it's around 16°C (50°F).
16 C
50 F

How to Grow Beetroot

Beetroot can be grown in a shady place. The seeds are easy to handle. Beetroot grows big leaves so they need space.

1. Get a wide pot- 40cm wide and 20cm deep or even bigger.

2. Fill it up with compost and firm it down gently.

3. Place the seeds one by one about 10-12cm apart.

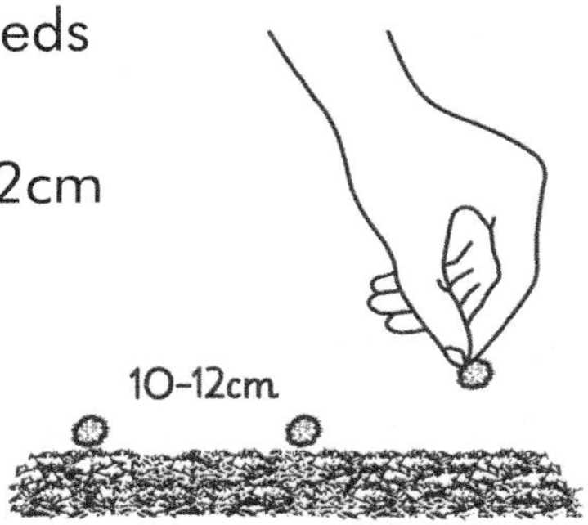

4. Cover the seeds with 2cm of compost and water well.

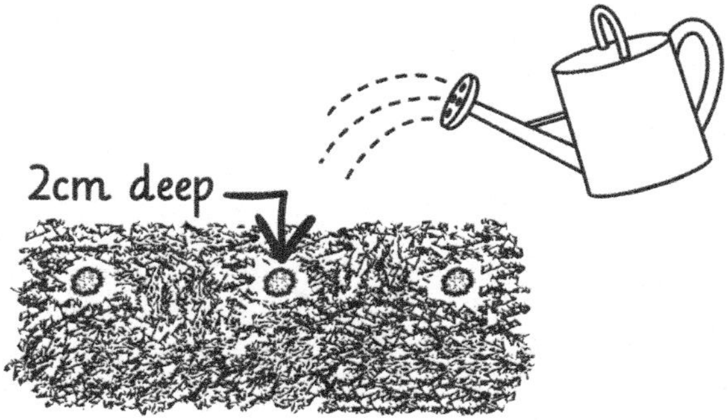

5. Beetroot loves water! Remember to water your beetroot plants regularly and keep the soil damp but not soggy.

Tips for Parents:

Explain the importance of spacing for healthy plant development. Make sure the pot has good drainage so the plants don't sit in soggy compost. Keep an eye on the beetroot in hot dry weather. Beetroot is a thirsty plant.

If peas were dancers, they'd be acrobats or ballerinas! They love to climb and twirl around garden supports, reaching for the sun.
HAP-PEA Circus
Pea plants are magicians for the soil. They take nitrogen from the air and turn it into food for other plants in the garden.
The *tallest* pea plant was 4.74m long!
Before we become peas, we bloom with beautiful edible flowers!

How to Grow Peas

Start peas indoors and move them outside when frost is gone. You can grow peas entirely indoors too.

1. Fill the pot with compost to the top and firm it gently.

2. Place the pea seeds about 5cm apart

3. Cover the seeds with a thin layer of compost and water them.

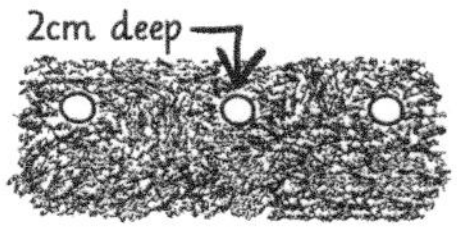

4. Seedlings will appear in two weeks.

Two Weeks Count

Keep the compost damp but not wet.

1 2 3 4 5 6 7

8 9 10 11 12 13 14

5. When you see flowers like these, start feeding the peas with organic plant food. Follow the instructions on the label and keep track in your book.

5. Water more regularly.

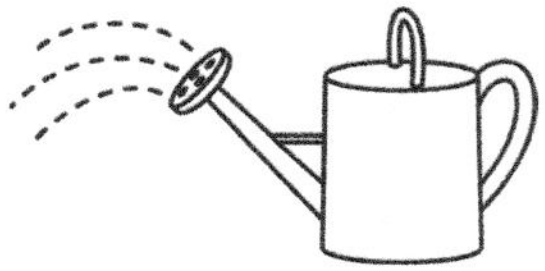

6. Give your peas support to climb on: trellis, canes, sticks, wire or netting.

Tips for Parents:

Discuss what type of peas to choose and what support they need. Together create the support for the peas. Encourage consistent record keeping in the book for watering and feeding. Teach your child when to pick the pods and how to shell the peas. You can harvest as mangetout or as peas. It is a 2 in 1 vegetable.

The longest runner bean pod measured 89.7cm; the heaviest pod weighed 196g and the largest runner bean leaf was 63.8cm x 67.7cm!
The World's *Tallest* Bean Plant was 14.1m. This is taller than two giraffes stacked on top of one another.
We love climbing. We always wind around canes anticlockwise.
We are Green beans but we can be yellow, purple, black and even speckled.

How to Grow Runner Beans

Runner beans get about 3m tall! They like a sunny spot protected from wind.

1. Fill three big heavy pots with compost.

2. Push a long cane into each pot and ask an adult to help you tie up the top ends of the canes. This is the wigwam for the plants to grow along.

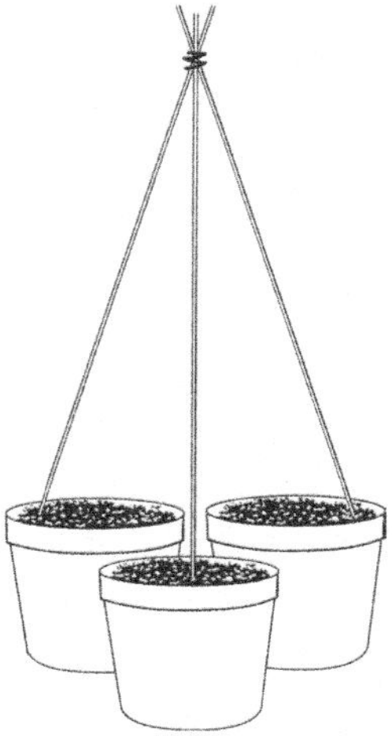

3. Next to each cane, make a small hole into the compost.

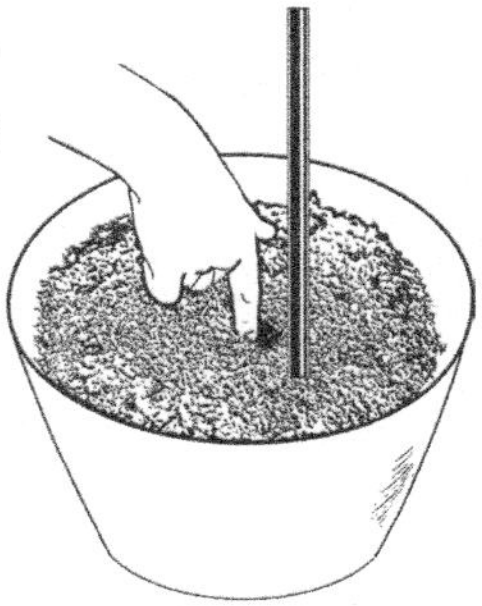

4. Place a seed into each hole and cover with compost.

5. Water the pots.

6. As the plants grow, water your runner beans every day, as they get very thirsty.

7. Pick your beans when they are about 20cm long. Do this every 2 days to keep them growing.

WARNING
DON'T EAT RAW
runner beans!

Tips for Parents:

If you grow runner beans in pots, it will be best to sow them in 3 or more heavy pots, each with cane in. Tie the tops of the canes together to make a teepee (wigwam). Remind your child to water the plants. Show them when and how to harvest. The seeds inside the pods can be dried and used in winter.

The *longest* cucumber was a bit longer than 113cm!
Cucumbers originated in India but now they grow all around the world.
We're made up mostly of water so we are super refreshing!
Gherkins are *small*, pickled cucumbers.

How to Grow Cucumbers

Choose a compact variety so you don't need canes. Grow one plant only in a big pot.

1. Fill up a small pot with compost and make a hole with your finger.

2. Place a cucumber seed on its side in the hole, cover with compost and water it well. Put the pot on a warm, sunny windowsill.

3. Keep the soil damp and watch the seedling growing. When you see roots coming out of the bottom of the pot, it needs a bigger pot.

4. Place the big pot in the sunniest spot and fill it with compost.

5. Water the plant in its small pot and gently take it out of the small pot. DON'T disturb the roots too much.

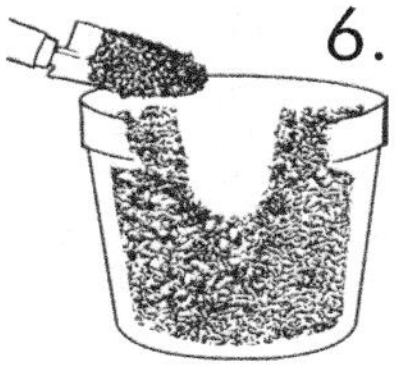

6. Make a hole in the compost as big as the small pot. Place the plant in the hole, bury the roots and firm the soil around them.

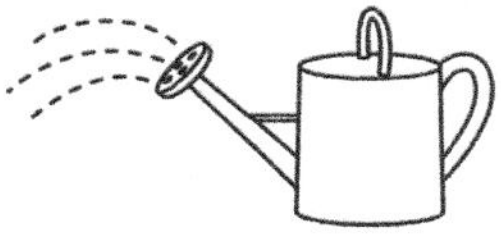

7. Water it well.

8. Cucumbers are very thirsty plants so water them regularly.

9. Feed your cucumber plants with plant food when they start making little cucumbers.

Tips for Parents:

Use a pot at least 40 cm deep and wide (30litres). Cucumbers are big on sunlight, water and nutrients. Remind your child to keep the soil evenly moist. Help your child keep track of feeding the plants.

1
2
3!
Long ago, people used turnips, not pumpkins!
I grew a large pumpkin, hollowed it out, climbed in it and paddled 25 miles!
WINNER: The Heaviest Pumpkin
2,749 pounds/1,246.9 kilograms
2023

How to Grow Pumpkins

Start your pumpkin plant indoors in a small pot. Soak the seeds in water overnight.

1. Fill up a small pot with compost. Make a 2cm deep hole with your finger.

2. Place a pumpkin seed on its side in the hole, cover with compost and water it well. Put the pot on a warm, sunny windowsill.

3. Keep the soil damp and watch the seedling growing until you see roots coming out of the bottom of the pot.

4. Get a big pot and place it in a sunny spot. Fill it with compost.

5. Dig a hole in the compost as big as the small pot.

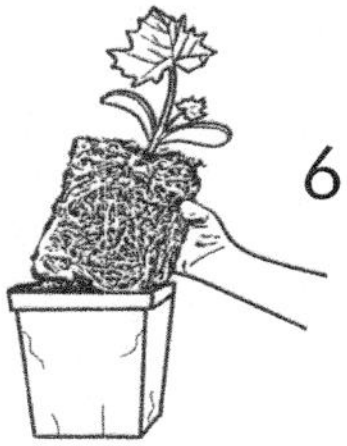

6. Water the pumpkin plant and gently take it out of the small pot.

7. Place it in the compost hole, bury the roots and firm the soil around them.

8. Water it regularly.

9. Be patient!
At Halloween, have fun carving the pumpkin you grew yourself!

Tips for Parents:

Choose a variety that is suited for growing in pots. Pumpkins love water, so remind your child to water the pot regularly. Protect young plants from slugs and snails and move pumpkin stems away from busy paths.

My Planting Log

Date

Today I planted ________

I planted it in

- ☐ a pot
- ☐ a grow bag
- ☐ the ground

Where did I put it? ________

Date

Today I planted ________

I planted it in

- ☐ a pot
- ☐ a grow bag
- ☐ the ground

Where did I put it? ________

Date

Today I planted ________

I planted it in

- ☐ a pot
- ☐ a grow bag
- ☐ the ground

Where did I put it? ________

Date

Today I planted ________

I planted it in

- ☐ a pot
- ☐ a grow bag
- ☐ the ground

Where did I put it? ________

My Planting Log

Date

Today I planted

I planted it in

- ☐ a pot
- ☐ a grow bag
- ☐ the ground

Where did I put it?

Date

Today I planted

I planted it in

- ☐ a pot
- ☐ a grow bag
- ☐ the ground

Where did I put it?

Date

Today I planted

I planted it in

- ☐ a pot
- ☐ a grow bag
- ☐ the ground

Where did I put it?

Date

Today I planted

I planted it in

- ☐ a pot
- ☐ a grow bag
- ☐ the ground

Where did I put it?

My Planting Log

Date

Today I planted ______

I planted it in

- ☐ a pot
- ☐ a grow bag
- ☐ the ground

Where did I put it? ______

Date

Today I planted ______

I planted it in

- ☐ a pot
- ☐ a grow bag
- ☐ the ground

Where did I put it? ______

Date

Today I planted ______

I planted it in

- ☐ a pot
- ☐ a grow bag
- ☐ the ground

Where did I put it? ______

Date

Today I planted ______

I planted it in

- ☐ a pot
- ☐ a grow bag
- ☐ the ground

Where did I put it? ______

My Planting Log

Date

Today I planted ______

I planted it in

- ☐ a pot
- ☐ a grow bag
- ☐ the ground

Where did I put it? ______

Date

Today I planted ______

I planted it in

- ☐ a pot
- ☐ a grow bag
- ☐ the ground

Where did I put it? ______

Date

Today I planted ______

I planted it in

- ☐ a pot
- ☐ a grow bag
- ☐ the ground

Where did I put it? ______

Date

Today I planted ______

I planted it in

- ☐ a pot
- ☐ a grow bag
- ☐ the ground

Where did I put it? ______

Daily Jobs

This part of the book is for keeping daily observations and recording the garden-related jobs, e.g. which plants were watered when, any weeds pulled out, protection from slug damage, feeding, what was the weather like, etc. Over time, looking back at these notes, your child will see how much work they have put into their garden which will create a sense of achievement and confidence.

How are my plants doing?

Once every week, encourage your child to observe closely how much their plants have grown and to draw a picture of what the plants look like. Teach them to observe carefully and draw what they can see. Then help your child to measure the plants' height. Teach them how to use a ruler or measuring tape if they don't know how to do it on their own. By drawing a picture of the plants every week, as well as recording the measurements, your child will be deepening their appreciation of nature, developing vital observational skills and practising patience. This is also a chance for you to spend quality time together, share your experience and facilitate powerful practical learning.

Deepening the learning

If you wish, you could take the measurement exercise further by posing simple prompts such as:

> *"How many days ago did you last measure it?"*
>
> *"I wonder how much the plant has grown since you last measured it."*

Be creative and take every opportunity to broaden your child's learning.

The reward for you as a parent will be amazing! You will witness your child's growth as an individual. By sharing in these gardening activities you are not just teaching them to grow food. You are developing their sense of wonder, responsibility, patience, perseverance and confidence. It is a journey that nurtures a lasting bond with the natural world.

Chapter 4 - Caring for the Plants
Garden tasks
Keep record
Daily jobs
Daily jobs
Keep record
Notice, observe
SNAILED IT
4

Caring for The Growing Plants

A week later, Sam and Mia had sown all the seeds they wanted and done all the planting.

Through the window, they saw Mr Parker on his way to his allotment. They ran outside to greet him.

Hello, Mr Parker!
What are you going to do in your garden today?

Mr Parker said that he checked on his plants every day.

"First, I stick my finger in the soil, about 2cm deep. If it feels dry I water the plants. If it is damp, I check again the next day.

I start feeding my plants with special food when they begin to bloom. This helps them grow healthy.

I also pull out any weeds, watch out for bugs, slugs or snails that may sneak in.

And then I record what I have done in my journal."

Sam and Mia thought, "Gardening is so interesting!"

The twins thanked Mr Parker and ran back home.

They knew what the next chapter of their Gardening Book was for - to record their garden jobs and tasks.

Look Mia!
We've got
"week" pages
in the book.

Each week
we can draw
pictures of our
plants, Sam!

My Daily Jobs

1st week

Monday ____________

The weather is

- [ ] I watered ____________
- [ ] I fed ____________
- [ ] I did something else :

Tuesday ____________

The weather is

- [ ] I watered ____________
- [ ] I fed ____________
- [ ] I did something else :

Wednesday ____________

The weather is

- [ ] I watered ____________
- [ ] I fed ____________
- [ ] I did something else :

Thursday ____________

The weather is

- [ ] I watered ____________
- [ ] I fed ____________
- [ ] I did something else :

Friday ________________

The weather is

- [ ] I watered ____________
- [ ] I fed ________________
- [ ] I did something else :

Saturday ________________

The weather is

- [ ] I watered ____________
- [ ] I fed ________________
- [ ] I did something else :

Sunday ________________

The weather is

- [ ] I watered ____________
- [ ] I fed ________________
- [ ] I did something else :

Notes:

How are my plants doing?

My plants look like this:

I wonder how tall they are ...

??

My Daily Jobs

2nd week

Monday ______________

The weather is

☐ I watered ______________

☐ I fed ______________

☐ I did something else :

Tuesday ______________

The weather is

☐ I watered ______________

☐ I fed ______________

☐ I did something else :

Wednesday ______________

The weather is

☐ I watered ______________

☐ I fed ______________

☐ I did something else :

Thursday ______________

The weather is

☐ I watered ______________

☐ I fed ______________

☐ I did something else :

Friday ____________________

The weather is

☐ I watered ____________

☐ I fed ________________

☐ I did something else :

Saturday ____________________

The weather is

☐ I watered ____________

☐ I fed ________________

☐ I did something else :

Sunday ____________________

The weather is

☐ I watered ____________

☐ I fed ________________

☐ I did something else :

Notes:

How are my plants doing?

My plants look like this:

I wonder how tall they are ...

My Daily Jobs

3rd week

Monday ____________

The weather is

☐ I watered ____________

☐ I fed ____________

☐ I did something else :

Tuesday ____________

The weather is

☐ I watered ____________

☐ I fed ____________

☐ I did something else :

Wednesday ____________

The weather is

☐ I watered ____________

☐ I fed ____________

☐ I did something else :

Thursday ____________

The weather is

☐ I watered ____________

☐ I fed ____________

☐ I did something else :

Friday ______________

The weather is

☐ I watered ___________

☐ I fed ______________

☐ I did something else :

Saturday ______________

The weather is

☐ I watered ___________

☐ I fed ______________

☐ I did something else :

Sunday ______________

The weather is

☐ I watered ___________

☐ I fed ______________

☐ I did something else :

Notes:

How are my plants doing?

My plants look like this:

I wonder how tall they are ...

My Daily Jobs

4th week

Monday ____________

The weather is

☐ I watered ____________

☐ I fed ____________

☐ I did something else :

Tuesday ____________

The weather is

☐ I watered ____________

☐ I fed ____________

☐ I did something else :

Wednesday ____________

The weather is

☐ I watered ____________

☐ I fed ____________

☐ I did something else :

Thursday ____________

The weather is

☐ I watered ____________

☐ I fed ____________

☐ I did something else :

Friday ______________

The weather is

☐ I watered ____________

☐ I fed ________________

☐ I did something else :

Saturday ______________

The weather is

☐ I watered ____________

☐ I fed ________________

☐ I did something else :

Sunday ______________

The weather is

☐ I watered ____________

☐ I fed ________________

☐ I did something else :

Notes:

How are my plants doing?

My plants look like this:

I wonder how tall they are ...

My Daily Jobs

5th week

Monday ____________

The weather is

- [ ] I watered ____________
- [ ] I fed ____________
- [ ] I did something else :

Tuesday ____________

The weather is

- [ ] I watered ____________
- [ ] I fed ____________
- [ ] I did something else :

Wednesday ____________

The weather is

- [ ] I watered ____________
- [ ] I fed ____________
- [ ] I did something else :

Thursday ____________

The weather is

- [ ] I watered ____________
- [ ] I fed ____________
- [ ] I did something else :

Friday ____________

The weather is

☐ I watered ____________

☐ I fed ____________

☐ I did something else :

Saturday ____________

The weather is

☐ I watered ____________

☐ I fed ____________

☐ I did something else :

Sunday ____________

The weather is

☐ I watered ____________

☐ I fed ____________

☐ I did something else :

Notes:

How are my plants doing?

My plants look like this:

I wonder how tall they are ... ??

My Daily Jobs

6th week

Monday ____________

The weather is

☐ I watered ____________

☐ I fed ____________

☐ I did something else :

Tuesday ____________

The weather is

☐ I watered ____________

☐ I fed ____________

☐ I did something else :

Wednesday ____________

The weather is

☐ I watered ____________

☐ I fed ____________

☐ I did something else :

Thursday ____________

The weather is

☐ I watered ____________

☐ I fed ____________

☐ I did something else :

Friday ____________________

The weather is

☐ I watered ______________

☐ I fed ____________________

☐ I did something else :

Saturday ________________

The weather is

☐ I watered ______________

☐ I fed ____________________

☐ I did something else :

Sunday __________________

The weather is

☐ I watered ______________

☐ I fed ____________________

☐ I did something else :

Notes:

How are my plants doing?

My plants look like this:

I wonder how tall they are ...

My Daily Jobs

7th week

Monday ________________

The weather is

☐ I watered ____________

☐ I fed ________________

☐ I did something else :

Tuesday ________________

The weather is

☐ I watered ____________

☐ I fed ________________

☐ I did something else :

Wednesday ____________

The weather is

☐ I watered ____________

☐ I fed ________________

☐ I did something else :

Thursday ______________

The weather is

☐ I watered ____________

☐ I fed ________________

☐ I did something else :

Friday ______________

The weather is

☐ I watered ______________

☐ I fed ______________

☐ I did something else :

Saturday ______________

The weather is

☐ I watered ______________

☐ I fed ______________

☐ I did something else :

Sunday ______________

The weather is

☐ I watered ______________

☐ I fed ______________

☐ I did something else :

Notes:

How are my plants doing?

My plants look like this:

I wonder how tall they are ... ??

My Daily Jobs

8th week

Monday ____________

The weather is

- [ ] I watered ____________
- [ ] I fed ____________
- [ ] I did something else :

Tuesday ____________

The weather is

- [ ] I watered ____________
- [ ] I fed ____________
- [ ] I did something else :

Wednesday ____________

The weather is

- [ ] I watered ____________
- [ ] I fed ____________
- [ ] I did something else :

Thursday ____________

The weather is

- [ ] I watered ____________
- [ ] I fed ____________
- [ ] I did something else :

Friday ______________

The weather is

☐ I watered ___________

☐ I fed ______________

☐ I did something else :

Saturday ______________

The weather is

☐ I watered ___________

☐ I fed ______________

☐ I did something else :

Sunday ______________

The weather is

☐ I watered ___________

☐ I fed ______________

☐ I did something else :

Notes:

How are my plants doing?

My plants look like this:

I wonder how tall they are ...

My Daily Jobs

9th week

Monday ______________

The weather is

- [ ] I watered ______________
- [ ] I fed ______________
- [ ] I did something else :

Tuesday ______________

The weather is

- [ ] I watered ______________
- [ ] I fed ______________
- [ ] I did something else :

Wednesday ______________

The weather is

- [ ] I watered ______________
- [ ] I fed ______________
- [ ] I did something else :

Thursday ______________

The weather is

- [ ] I watered ______________
- [ ] I fed ______________
- [ ] I did something else :

Friday ____________________

The weather is

☐ I watered ____________

☐ I fed ________________

☐ I did something else :

Sunday ________________

The weather is

☐ I watered ____________

☐ I fed ________________

☐ I did something else :

Saturday ________________

The weather is

☐ I watered ____________

☐ I fed ________________

☐ I did something else :

Notes:

How are my plants doing?

My plants look like this:

I wonder how tall they are ...

My Daily Jobs

10th week

Monday ____________

The weather is

☐ I watered ____________

☐ I fed ____________

☐ I did something else :

Tuesday ____________

The weather is

☐ I watered ____________

☐ I fed ____________

☐ I did something else :

Wednesday ____________

The weather is

☐ I watered ____________

☐ I fed ____________

☐ I did something else :

Thursday ____________

The weather is

☐ I watered ____________

☐ I fed ____________

☐ I did something else :

Friday ____________

The weather is

- [ ] I watered ____________
- [ ] I fed ____________
- [ ] I did something else :

Saturday ____________

The weather is

- [ ] I watered ____________
- [ ] I fed ____________
- [ ] I did something else :

Sunday ____________

The weather is

- [ ] I watered ____________
- [ ] I fed ____________
- [ ] I did something else :

Notes:

How are my plants doing?

My plants look like this:

I wonder how tall they are ...

My Daily Jobs

11th week

Monday ______________

The weather is

- [ ] I watered ______________
- [ ] I fed ______________
- [ ] I did something else :

Tuesday ______________

The weather is

- [ ] I watered ______________
- [ ] I fed ______________
- [ ] I did something else :

Wednesday ______________

The weather is

- [ ] I watered ______________
- [ ] I fed ______________
- [ ] I did something else :

Thursday ______________

The weather is

- [ ] I watered ______________
- [ ] I fed ______________
- [ ] I did something else :

Friday ____________________

The weather is

☐ I watered ______________

☐ I fed ____________________

☐ I did something else :

Saturday ________________

The weather is

☐ I watered ______________

☐ I fed ____________________

☐ I did something else :

Sunday __________________

The weather is

☐ I watered ______________

☐ I fed ____________________

☐ I did something else :

Notes:

How are my plants doing?

My plants look like this:

I wonder how tall they are ...

??

My Daily Jobs

12th week

Monday ____________

The weather is

☐ I watered ____________

☐ I fed ____________

☐ I did something else :

Tuesday ____________

The weather is

☐ I watered ____________

☐ I fed ____________

☐ I did something else :

Wednesday ____________

The weather is

☐ I watered ____________

☐ I fed ____________

☐ I did something else :

Thursday ____________

The weather is

☐ I watered ____________

☐ I fed ____________

☐ I did something else :

Friday ____________________

The weather is

☐ I watered ____________

☐ I fed ________________

☐ I did something else :

Saturday ________________

The weather is

☐ I watered ____________

☐ I fed ________________

☐ I did something else :

Sunday __________________

The weather is

☐ I watered ____________

☐ I fed ________________

☐ I did something else :

Notes:

How are my plants doing?

My plants look like this:

I wonder how tall they are ...

??

My Daily Jobs

13th week

Monday ______________

The weather is

- [ ] I watered ____________
- [ ] I fed ________________
- [ ] I did something else :

Tuesday ______________

The weather is

- [ ] I watered ____________
- [ ] I fed ________________
- [ ] I did something else :

Wednesday ____________

The weather is

- [ ] I watered ____________
- [ ] I fed ________________
- [ ] I did something else :

Thursday _____________

The weather is

- [ ] I watered ____________
- [ ] I fed ________________
- [ ] I did something else :

Friday ____________________

The weather is

☐ I watered ______________

☐ I fed ____________________

☐ I did something else :

Saturday ________________

The weather is

☐ I watered ______________

☐ I fed ____________________

☐ I did something else :

Sunday __________________

The weather is

☐ I watered ______________

☐ I fed ____________________

☐ I did something else :

Notes:

How are my plants doing?

My plants look like this:

I wonder how tall they are ...

??

My Daily Jobs

14th week

Monday ______________

The weather is

☐ I watered ____________

☐ I fed ________________

☐ I did something else :

Tuesday ______________

The weather is

☐ I watered ____________

☐ I fed ________________

☐ I did something else :

Wednesday ____________

The weather is

☐ I watered ____________

☐ I fed ________________

☐ I did something else :

Thursday ____________

The weather is

☐ I watered ____________

☐ I fed ________________

☐ I did something else :

Friday ______________

The weather is

☐ I watered ____________

☐ I fed ________________

☐ I did something else :

Saturday ______________

The weather is

☐ I watered ____________

☐ I fed ________________

☐ I did something else :

Sunday ______________

The weather is

☐ I watered ____________

☐ I fed ________________

☐ I did something else :

Notes:

How are my plants doing?

My plants look like this:

I wonder how tall they are ...

??

My Daily Jobs

15th week

Monday ______________

The weather is

- [ ] I watered ______________
- [ ] I fed ______________
- [ ] I did something else :

Tuesday ______________

The weather is

- [ ] I watered ______________
- [ ] I fed ______________
- [ ] I did something else :

Wednesday ______________

The weather is

- [ ] I watered ______________
- [ ] I fed ______________
- [ ] I did something else :

Thursday ______________

The weather is

- [ ] I watered ______________
- [ ] I fed ______________
- [ ] I did something else :

Friday ______________

The weather is

☐ I watered ______________

☐ I fed ______________

☐ I did something else :

Saturday ______________

The weather is

☐ I watered ______________

☐ I fed ______________

☐ I did something else :

Sunday ______________

The weather is

☐ I watered ______________

☐ I fed ______________

☐ I did something else :

Notes:

How are my plants doing?

My plants look like this:

I wonder how tall they are ...

??

My Daily Jobs

16th week

Monday ______________

The weather is

☐ I watered ______________

☐ I fed ______________

☐ I did something else :

Tuesday ______________

The weather is

☐ I watered ______________

☐ I fed ______________

☐ I did something else :

Wednesday ______________

The weather is

☐ I watered ______________

☐ I fed ______________

☐ I did something else :

Thursday ______________

The weather is

☐ I watered ______________

☐ I fed ______________

☐ I did something else :

Friday ____________________

The weather is

☐ I watered ______________

☐ I fed ____________________

☐ I did something else :

Saturday ________________

The weather is

☐ I watered ______________

☐ I fed ____________________

☐ I did something else :

Sunday __________________

The weather is

☐ I watered ______________

☐ I fed ____________________

☐ I did something else :

Notes:

How are my plants doing?

My plants look like this:

I wonder how tall they are ...

My Daily Jobs

17th week

Monday ______________

The weather is

☐ I watered ______________

☐ I fed ______________

☐ I did something else :

Tuesday ______________

The weather is

☐ I watered ______________

☐ I fed ______________

☐ I did something else :

Wednesday ______________

The weather is

☐ I watered ______________

☐ I fed ______________

☐ I did something else :

Thursday ______________

The weather is

☐ I watered ______________

☐ I fed ______________

☐ I did something else :

Friday ____________________

The weather is

- [ ] I watered ______________
- [ ] I fed ____________________
- [ ] I did something else :

Saturday ________________

The weather is

- [ ] I watered ______________
- [ ] I fed ____________________
- [ ] I did something else :

Sunday __________________

The weather is

- [ ] I watered ______________
- [ ] I fed ____________________
- [ ] I did something else :

Notes:

How are my plants doing?

My plants look like this:

I wonder how tall they are ...

??

My Daily Jobs

18th week

Monday ______________

The weather is

☐ I watered ____________

☐ I fed ________________

☐ I did something else :

Tuesday ______________

The weather is

☐ I watered ____________

☐ I fed ________________

☐ I did something else :

Wednesday ______________

The weather is

☐ I watered ____________

☐ I fed ________________

☐ I did something else :

Thursday ______________

The weather is

☐ I watered ____________

☐ I fed ________________

☐ I did something else :

Friday ______________

The weather is

- [ ] I watered ____________
- [ ] I fed ______________
- [ ] I did something else :

Saturday ______________

The weather is

- [ ] I watered ____________
- [ ] I fed ______________
- [ ] I did something else :

Sunday ______________

The weather is

- [ ] I watered ____________
- [ ] I fed ______________
- [ ] I did something else :

Notes:

How are my plants doing?

My plants look like this:

I wonder how tall they are ...

??

My Daily Jobs

19th week

Monday ____________

The weather is

- [ ] I watered ____________
- [ ] I fed ____________
- [ ] I did something else :

Tuesday ____________

The weather is

- [ ] I watered ____________
- [ ] I fed ____________
- [ ] I did something else :

Wednesday ____________

The weather is

- [ ] I watered ____________
- [ ] I fed ____________
- [ ] I did something else :

Thursday ____________

The weather is

- [ ] I watered ____________
- [ ] I fed ____________
- [ ] I did something else :

Friday ____________________

The weather is

☐ I watered ______________

☐ I fed ____________________

☐ I did something else :

Saturday ____________________

The weather is

☐ I watered ______________

☐ I fed ____________________

☐ I did something else :

Sunday ____________________

The weather is

☐ I watered ______________

☐ I fed ____________________

☐ I did something else :

Notes:

How are my plants doing?

My plants look like this:

I wonder how tall they are ...

??

My Daily Jobs

20th week

Monday ______________

The weather is

- [ ] I watered ______________
- [ ] I fed ______________
- [ ] I did something else :

Tuesday ______________

The weather is

- [ ] I watered ______________
- [ ] I fed ______________
- [ ] I did something else :

Wednesday ______________

The weather is

- [ ] I watered ______________
- [ ] I fed ______________
- [ ] I did something else :

Thursday ______________

The weather is

- [ ] I watered ______________
- [ ] I fed ______________
- [ ] I did something else :

Friday ______________

The weather is

☐ I watered ______________

☐ I fed ______________

☐ I did something else :

Saturday ______________

The weather is

☐ I watered ______________

☐ I fed ______________

☐ I did something else :

Sunday ______________

The weather is

☐ I watered ______________

☐ I fed ______________

☐ I did something else :

Notes:

How are my plants doing?

My plants look like this:

I wonder how tall they are ...

??

As young green thumbs delve into the world of growing plants, they are bound to encounter some challenges with pests. These challenges provide excellent opportunities for learning and growth. Here, we'll explore common garden pests and discuss ways you can support your young gardener in protecting their plants.

Snails and slugs are notorious for nibbling on tender leaves, leaving behind a slimy trail of destruction. Encourage your child to set up barriers. They could sprinkle crushed eggshells around the plants, apply Vaseline or attach copper tape around the pots' rims. These materials create obstacles that snails and slugs find challenging to cross. Additionally, a night-time garden inspection with a torch can help catch them in the act.

The larval stage of butterflies, ***caterpillars,*** can be voracious eaters. Teach your young gardener to inspect the underside of leaves for tiny butterfly eggs and remove them by hand.

In some cases, furry intruders like ***rabbits*** can pose a significant threat to a garden. Fencing is an effective solution. Together, choose aesthetically pleasing fencing to protect the plants. Additionally, planting strong-smelling herbs like mint or lavender around the garden can deter rabbits and other wildlife.

Birds also need restrictions. Consider using bird netting to protect fruits and tender plants. Encourage placing bird feeders away from the garden to redirect their attention.

Teach your young gardener about ***companion planting*** – the strategic placement of plants that benefit each other. For instance, basil improves tomato flavour and the strong scent of basil leaves also deters aphids. A perfect partnership in the kitchen too!

It's essential to approach pest challenges with a ***positive mindset.*** Encourage your child to view these experiences as opportunities to learn more about the natural world and how ecosystems work. Explain that even seasoned gardeners face pest issues and the key is to adapt and find sustainable solutions.

Help your young gardener explore ***natural remedies*** to control pests. Neem oil, garlic spray and soapy water solutions are effective and safe alternatives to chemical pesticides. Involving your child in the process of making these remedies can make it an exciting and educational experience.

Remember, gardening is a journey filled with valuable lessons. By guiding your young gardener through the challenges of pest management, you're not only nurturing their green skills but also instilling resilience, problem-solving and a deep appreciation for the wonders of nature.

Chapter 5 - Wildlife
Wildlife
Wildlife
Wildlife
Wildlife
Wildlife
Wildlife
5

Wildlife Chompers

It rained during the night.

In the morning, Sam and Mia noticed unusual holes in the leaves of the lettuces. Something had nibbled on them during the night!

The twins had to investigate.

When it got dark, they grabbed their torches and headed into the garden to find out who was making the holes in the leaves.

Soon they discovered the little culprits – slugs and snails were sneakily enjoying a feast on their plants!

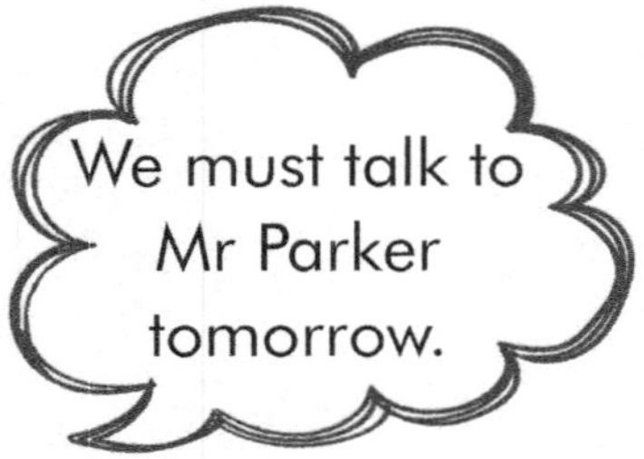
We must talk to Mr Parker tomorrow.

Mum and Dad suggested they pick up the slugs and snails, put them in an empty pot, take them far away and drop them there.

Mr Parker explained that every gardener must learn how to protect their plants from the wildlife.

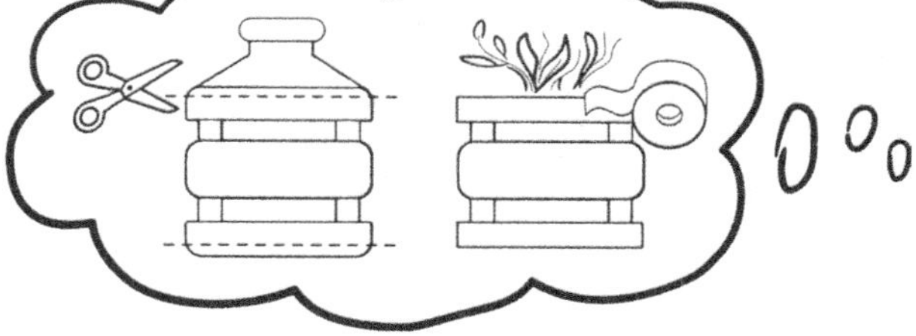

In my garden I set up slug barriers with plastic bottles and copper tape.

Vaseline
But I have a much better idea for you!

"Smear some Vaseline around the top of the plant pots. Use a kitchen paper towel and your finger," Mr Parker smiled.

"Caterpillars, aphids, ants, woodlice, birds, rabbits, deer, mice, rats," he continued, "all like to have a nibble at your tasty plants. You must become very clever at stopping them."

Sam and Mia started thinking of clever ways to protect their garden. They became very observant and recorded in the Wildlife Log the creatures they spotted in their garden.

What wildlife have I seen in my garden?

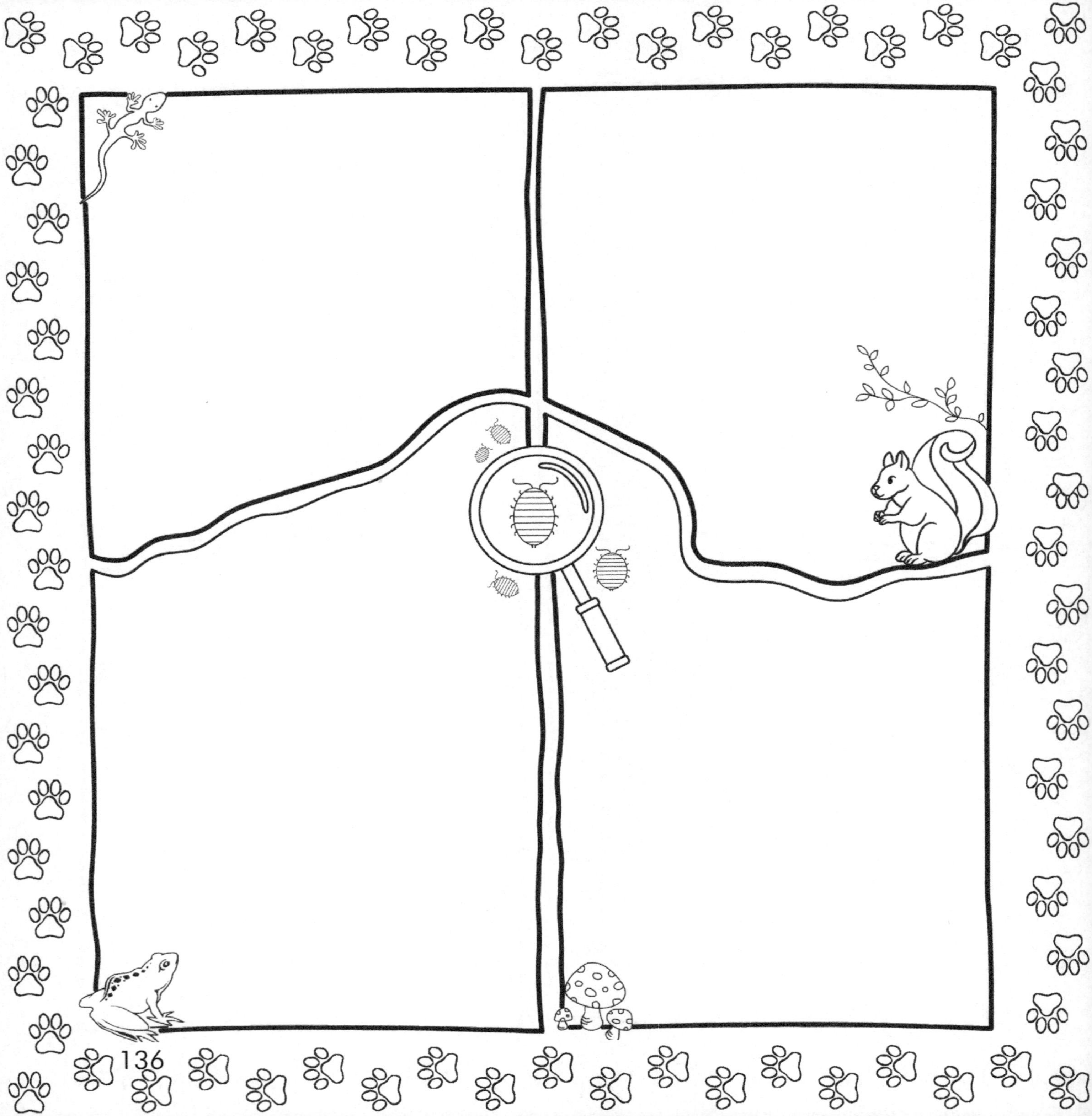

This chapter is for exploring the joy of slowing down and appreciating the moment. It's about helping your child notice and enjoy the beauty of nature right on their doorstep. The pages in this chapter serve as a special space for capturing memorable moments, inviting your young gardener to draw pictures or stick photos of enchanting discoveries amidst the greenery. These pages serve as a "personal canvas" for your child to express their unique connection with the garden.

Encouraging your child to engage in this creative documentation deepens their bond with nature and provides a tangible record of their journey as garden explorers. Each drawing or photo becomes a cherished memory, a testament to the joy found in the simplicity of the garden. Over time, during the growing season, these pages will become a celebration of various discoveries, offering a visual diary for your child to revisit, share and reflect upon.

Here are some ***suggestions*** to facilitate this mindful practice for your child:

Unstructured Exploration

Allow your child to enjoy the garden without a strict plan. This makes room for spontaneous discoveries.

Quiet Observation

Prompt your child to sit quietly, observing the details of plants, insects and the surrounding world.

Listen to Nature's Symphony

Take a moment to listen to the sounds of the garden – the rustling leaves, chirping birds, buzzing insects etc.

Close-Eye Listening

Ask your child to close their eyes and really listen to the different sounds of nature. This is an opportunity for a deeper connection.

Cloud Gazing

On sunny days, gaze at the clouds in the sky, encouraging your child to use their imagination and create stories with the shapes they see in the clouds.

Express Gratitude

Foster a sense of gratitude by encouraging your child to express thanks for the things they enjoy in the garden. It could be small things or it could be big things.

As you record these memorable moments and exciting discoveries, the following pages will become an illustration of your child's unique connection with the natural world. Happy creating!

6

Magic Everywhere

One afternoon, after a refreshing rain shower, Sam and Mia looked up and saw a bright, colourful rainbow in the sky.

It made everything feel a bit magical!

Excited, they took out their Gardening Book and started drawing a picture of the rainbow.

Sam even wrote some words about the pretty colours in the sky.

The next day the twins noticed that their cherry tomato plant had opened its first flower! Sam and Mia drew pictures of the tiny, delicate blossom and put the date on it too.

What other magical things can you discover, kiddos?

The twins decided to explore.
They started looking for interesting things.

They found ladybirds hiding in the leaves,

silky spider's webs,

a bird family nesting in a tree...

Each time they found something special, they recorded it in their Gardening Book.

Gradually, the twins realised that the more they looked for magic, the more magic they found!

Their small garden was full of wonderful surprises, and they could find something special every day.

The Gardening Book soon filled up with their pictures and stories. It turned into a book of happiness and wonder.

Magic Moments To reMember

Magic Moments To reMember

Magic Moments To reMember

Magic Moments To reMember

Magic Moments To reMember

Magic Moments To reMember

Magic Moments To reMember

Magic Moments To reMember

Magic Moments To reMember

Magic Moments To reMember

Magic Moments To reMember

Magic Moments To reMember

Magic Moments To reMember

Magic Moments To reMember

Magic Moments To reMember

Magic Moments To reMember

Magic Moments To reMember

Magic Moments To reMember

Magic Moments To reMember

Magic Moments To reMember

This chapter, "Games, Crafts and Stories", has been included in My First Gardening Book to keep children engaged in play, creativity and learning while patiently awaiting the growth and harvest of their garden plants.

The chapter features 10 stories for adults to read to children. Each story is accompanied by its own colouring page. This shared storytelling not only boosts imagination but also enriches vocabulary and helps with focus and concentration. Children learn to love reading by being read to. This shared time together also strengthens the bond between you and your little gardener.

After each story, your child has an opportunity to explore a variety of puzzles, games and crafts. We have tried our best to relate these activities to the story narrative and to create an environment for discussing the valuable lessons learned in the stories. These nature-connected activities encourage your child to explore new concepts, learn new things and develop problem-solving skills, all while having fun.

We have added extra guidance for adults in the form of tips, insights and suggestions, ensuring every moment spent in the garden or outside of it is both enjoyable and educational. May "Games, Crafts and Stories" be a source of joy, discovery and growth for your young gardener.

Chapter 7 - Games, Crafts and Stories

Games, Crafts and Stories

While waiting for their plants to grow, Sam and Mia had lots of fun.

One day they played "Scavenger hunt".

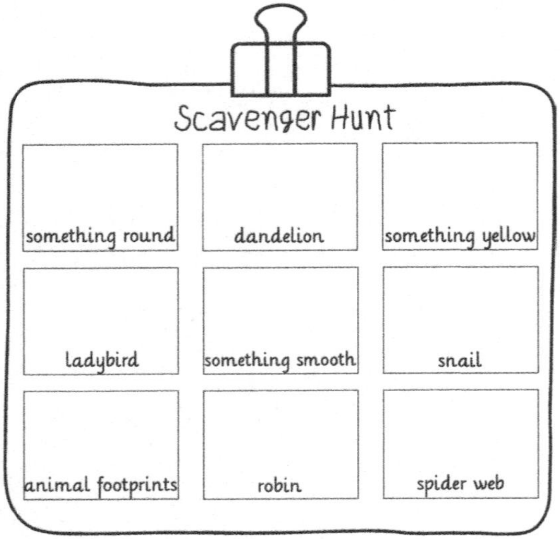

Their mum made up a list of items for them to find: a round pebble, a feather, three kinds of leaves and other things. Then Sam and Mia dashed around the garden searching high and low.

It was so much fun!

Another day their mum read them a story, and the twins decided to make art with leaves.

Their Gardening Book was full of so many interesting stories, games and topics to explore!

The twins loved stargazing with their dad and started writing notes to each other in a secret code!

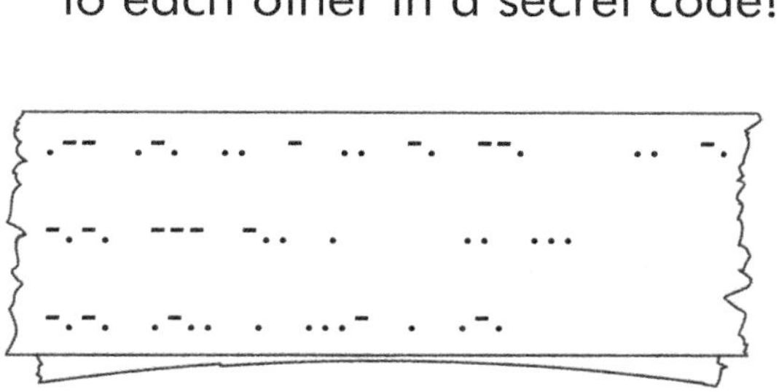

They understood that some things require time, persistence and patience.

Sam and Mia realised that their garden wasn't just for growing veggies. It was for learning about life too.

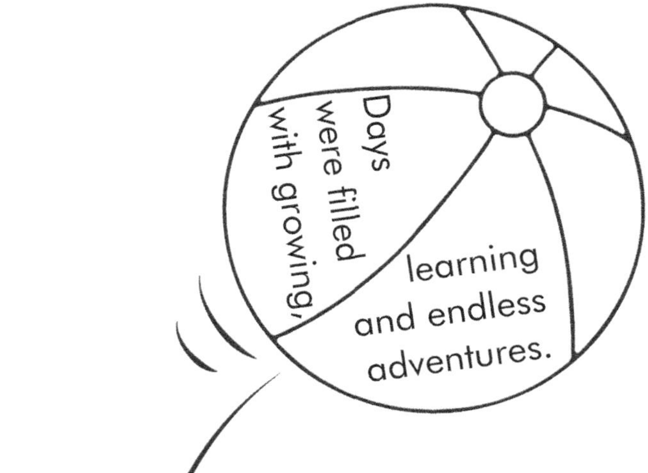

The garden taught them about perseverance, respect and sharing with others.

They found out that every plant, every bug and every bird had its own story to tell, if they were listening.

And they were now...

The Determined Little Caterpillar

In a vibrant garden lived Cali, a caterpillar with a passion for delightful bites. Her dream was to visit Butterfly Valley, a place rumoured to boast the most scrumptious greenery. Excited, determined and driven by her desire for extraordinary tastes, Cali embarked on her journey.

On Monday, Cali came upon a dense patch of tall grass blocking her path. Undeterred, she pushed through. The anticipation of reaching Butterfly Valley kept her going.

On Tuesday, a wide stream appeared, seemingly impossible to cross. Cali explored the bank and found a sturdy log bridging the stream. Determined, she carefully crawled along the log, balancing her way to the other side.

On Wednesday, another obstacle arose—a tangle of roots formed a barrier in her path. Cali took a moment to think and then wriggled her way through the gaps without losing her resolve. Her hunger for the delectable plants drove her onward.

On Thursday, time pressed upon her. A strong wind blew across the garden. Seeking cover, Cali refused to give up on her journey. Her eagerness now transformed into an even stronger determination to feast on the rumoured delights.

On Friday, exhaustion overcame her. Recognizing the need for rest, Cali found a cosy spot among some broad leaves and spun a silky cocoon to snuggle in. Deep within her cocoon, she dreamt of the sumptuous flavours that awaited her.

Emerging on Saturday, Cali began learning how to use her beautiful new wings. Soon, she mastered flying which was better than crawling, she thought. Just then, to her utter amazement, flying high above the ground, she discovered she was in Butterfly Valley.

Cali's metamorphosis was profound. On Sunday, she understood that her journey was not just about reaching the Valley but realising that she had been surrounded by the most delightful food the entire time. Now, as a magnificent butterfly, she could appreciate every corner of the Valley freely.

Cali's dream had come true in the most unexpected and flavoursome way. Gratitude and appreciation filled her heart as she embraced the delectable paradise she had taken for granted, learning a valuable lesson that sometimes what we seek elsewhere is right in our own back garden and that the grass isn't always greener on the other side—sometimes, what we seek is right under our nose, we just need to learn how to see it.

* * *

Did you ever really want something but then discovered you already had something super cool that made you just as happy?

Make a Caterpillar *

Cut* an eggs box in half lengthwise so that you have two long bumpy caterpillar bodies.

Paint the caterpillar's body using your favourite colours.

Add eyes and a mouth.

Make* two holes at the top of the caterpillar's head.

Poke two pipe cleaners through the holes and twist them into antennae.

Bug Safari

Become a bug detective in your garden!

Lift rocks, look under leaves, search in flower beds. When you find a bug, like a beetle or a spider, you can draw a picture of it and try to figure out what it's called. If you don't know, ask your parents to help you look it up.

Nature Pictures

You could make a picture using natural materials. It could be a face, a patten or anything else you like to make.

Nature Engineering

Can you build a bridge using only natural materials?
Can your bridge hold your favourite toy without collapsing?

Buzzy Bee is decorating her honeycomb using a number pattern. Can you help her?

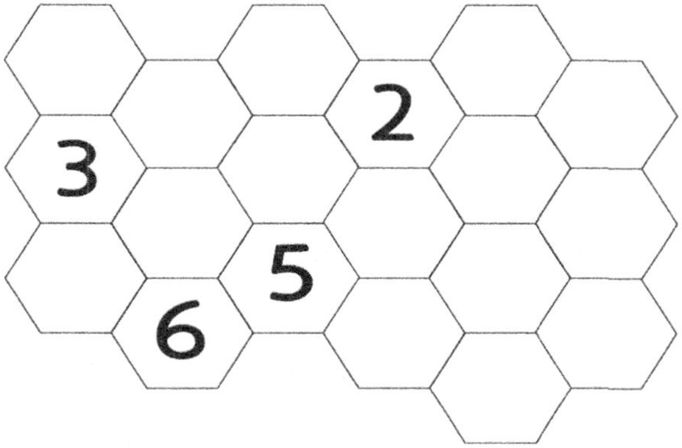

TIP: Look for the number pattern

Origami

In Japanese, **ori** means *folding;* **kami** means *paper*.

Challenge yourself to make an origami butterfly, a caterpillar or a bee. You could watch a video to show you how to do it.

Tips for Parents

* Help your child with the cutting and making of holes in the Caterpillar craft.

Take a picture of your child's creations and remind them to add their pictures to the Magic Moments to reMember.

Grinn, The Garden Gnome

In a charming garden, surrounded by towering trees and colourful flowers, a community of gnomes lived together. They all wore colourful hats, sported rosy cheeks and had big blue eyes, taking pride in their similar appearances.

Among them was Grinn, a gnome who often felt a bit different. He would sit at the garden's edge, aware of his baggy, green trousers.

One sunny day, a joyful butterfly noticed that Grinn was sitting alone in contemplation. The butterfly landed on his shoulder and asked, "What's on your mind, Grinn?"

Grinn sighed, "I feel like I don't fit in. All the other gnomes look so smart and shiny. I'm the odd one out! I wish I looked the same as them. They always single me out and laugh at me, making fun of my baggy trousers. That's why I sit alone at the edge of the garden."

"But Grinn," said the butterfly, "the garden wouldn't be a fun place if we all looked the same... The garden is special because everything is different. We all have our own uniqueness."

Grinn pondered on this and decided to explore around. To his surprise, birds, ladybirds, frogs, rabbits and squirrels each had their own unique traits. Ladybirds had different spots, birds sang different tunes, frogs displayed various patterns and colours, rabbits had ears of varied length, and no two squirrels had the same size bushy tail. They were all content being themselves and had no desire to be like others.

Gradually, Grinn realized that it didn't matter what clothes he wore or what his gnome hat looked like. He discovered he had a talent for telling funny stories and making others laugh! "I help to make the world a happier place!" he exclaimed.

When Grinn returned home, the other gnomes were overjoyed! They had missed Grinn's presence. It just wasn't the same without him and there was a gaping hole in his absence. Everyone wanted to know where he had been and what he'd been up to. They all agreed Grinn brought cheer and laughter and decided to make a special place for him right in the middle of the garden. The gnomes appreciated Grinn's jokes and they all began to see the beauty in being different, just like the diverse creatures Grinn had met. The gnomes stopped competing with each other and started living in harmony, appreciating their unique gifts and talents.

The garden became an even more joyful place with cooperation and mutual respect, as Grinn learned a very special lesson — be yourself and help others by doing what you love.

* * *

What unique talent or trait do you think you have that makes you special?

Why do you think it's cool to be yourself instead of trying to be like someone else?

Painted Rocks

These are little pieces of art you can make for your garden or for presents. Find smooth rocks and then paint them with bright colours and fun designs. You can make them look like tiny characters to guard your garden or you can paint pretty patterns on them. After the paint dries out, you can place them in your garden to make it even more beautiful and special.

Garden Memory Game

Draw pairs of pictures of things from your garden such as flowers, insects, plants, tools, etc. Mix them up and turn them all face down. Take turns flipping two cards over. If they match, you keep them. If not, flip them back and remember where they are for next time. The person with the most pairs wins the game! This game is a great exercise for your brain and memory.

Daisy Chains

There are different ways to make daisy chains.

One way is by cutting a slit in one stem and threading another stem through. Thicker stems are best for this method.

Another way is to use braiding. This method is best if the stems are long and flexible. You could practise braiding with string before you move on to daisies.

Wind-Powered Creations

Do you know how much fun flying a kite is? It's even better flying the kite that you made yourself!

You can also build wind chimes for the garden and a windmill toy to play with. Have a go, try out these activities.

Tips for Parents

Help with any heavy lifting/ tying/ cutting while your child is making their kite/ windmill/ wind chimes, etc.

Take pictures of your child's creations for the Magic Moments to reMember part of the book.

Badger's New Perspective

In the midst of Happy Meadow, badger Bernard found himself in a bit of a pickle. The meadow had some new residents: a group of playful moles led by the adventurous Monty. The moles loved digging and creating tunnels that criss-crossed the ground and they even accidentally burrowed into Bernard's home which was also made of tunnels. This made Bernard very upset: he liked his space neat and tidy so he couldn't help but get annoyed by all the mole activity.

Every day, Bernard argued with Monty about the moles' burrows. He would stomp around, shouting that the meadow was his home, and that the moles were destroying it. The moles on the other hand couldn't understand what Bernard was talking about. They thought their holes made the meadow interesting; the rabbits even asked them to dig them a special hole!

While Bernard argued, the other meadow animals seemed fine with the moles. Birds chirped, rabbits hopped, butterflies fluttered about undisturbed by the moles' activities.

One sunny day, Bernard took a break from arguing. He sat by his burrow and watched the other animals going about their business, not minding the moles one bit. It got Bernard thinking – it seemed he was the only one getting upset. He was tired of being angry. He decided to change his perspective.

Instead of grumbling at the moles, Bernard began focusing on his own business. He started enjoying his own activities: he dug for tasty grubs, rolled in the soft grass and even tried a bit of stargazing. To his surprise, the meadow felt happier, and Bernard felt happier too. Bernard started to see that the moles contribute to the meadow life, and he often found lots of grubs in the soil that the moles had dug out of the ground, making his food gathering easier.

The moles noticed Bernard's change. They started to get along with him, and even said "Hello" and "Good morning" as they went about their business. Do you know what happened next? The moles moved to a different part of the meadow- after all, there was more than enough meadow for everyone to live together.

The Happy Meadow became even more wonderful with all the different creatures living together, each one with their own special talent contributing to the harmony of nature. With a big smile on his face, Bernard realised that sharing and accepting others made the meadow a better place for everyone.

The tale of Bernard and Monty became a favourite bedtime story for the young ones in Happy Meadow, teaching them that sometimes, when we stop getting upset and worrying about what others are doing, magic happens and everything falls into place. This is how Bernard learned that we are all different and there is a place on this planet for each and every one of us.

Stargazing

Once upon a time, curious minds studied the night sky and connected the stars with imaginary lines to create amazing shapes called *constellations*. One such constellation is called the *Big Dipper.* People crafted stories about the constellations to help with remembering them better. By observing the stars at night, skilled captains could decide which way to sail their ships.

If you're up for an adventure, grab a blanket, get a star map or download a stargazing App and head outside to explore. Lay down and start exploring the constellations. You could even get a telescope or binoculars for an even closer look. Make it a fun night out with snacks and drinks and dive into the universe of stories waiting for you to explore!

Tip: A small torch can be handy.

Make a Spirograph Toy

Have you heard of a Spirograph?

It's a cool toy that draws looping designs. It is made of a small disc that goes inside a bigger circle. There are a few holes in the small disc. You put your pencil tip into one of these holes and you draw while moving the small disc around the inside of the bigger circle. This way you can create amazing looping patterns.

You can make your own spirograph at home. Just find some rubber bands and two lids: a large lid and a small plastic lid that you can make a few holes* in. Ask an adult for help!

Check out the instructions on the next page and happy drawing!

Carefully move the small lid around the inside of the big lid. Let the small lid spin as it goes.
Keep going around and around until you return to the start of your line.

Spirograph toy

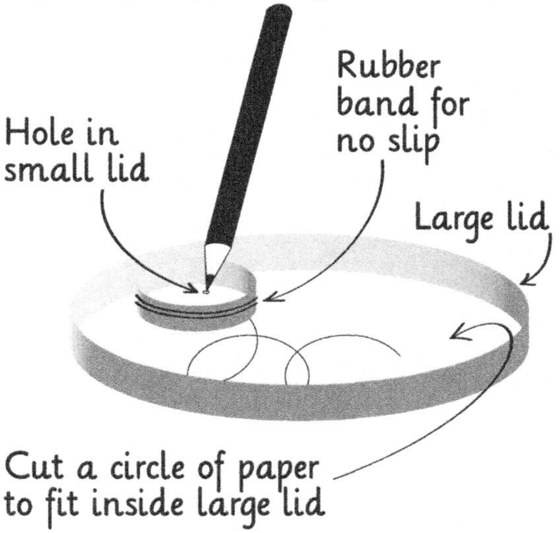

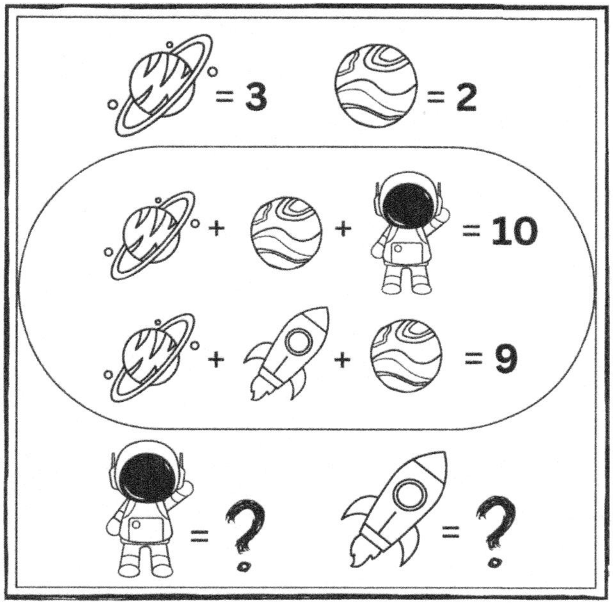

Tips for Parents

Downloading a stargazing App and together study the sky and the stars.

* For the toy, suggest lids of appropriate sizes. It's best if the small lid is made from soft plastic so it's easier to poke holes in it. Help your child with the making of the holes.

Flint Found Courage in Fear

Once upon a time, nestled In the heart of a big forest, in a cosy burrow, lived a bunny family. The youngest among them was a shy bunny named Flint. He was the smallest, the fluffiest and the most timid of all the other bunny kids in the family.

One day, Flint and his siblings decided to explore a little bit further away than usual. Hopping about and chasing each other around, they ventured into terrain they didn't know well, and Flint, being the youngest, tripped over a gnarled old tree root and tumbled down a seemingly never-ending slope. Eventually, he came to a stop, battered, bruised and covered in leaves.

In a panic, young Flint rushed to find his way back home but got more and more terrified by his own rustling noises, his imagination running wild about the scary things that might be lurking in the shadows. Completely petrified, Flint shouted for help. His voice echoed through the trees. No one answered, which made him even more frightened.

Suddenly, to his left, there was a gentle rustle, followed by these words, "Hey, little one. You're making a bit of a disturbance, are you lost? I'm Tina. Don't be afraid!" Then an old wise rabbit came into view. She had a very soothing, gentle voice which instantly calmed Flint. "Why don't we sit down on this old log, and see if I can help you," the old rabbit said.

Listening to Tina's comforting words, Flint started to feel a bit better. She shared that in her youth, she had also faced fears and uncertainties but she had learned how to face them. "It's okay to be scared, dear. Let us do some deep breathing together. This always seems to help. You're not alone. You're quicker and stronger than you think. Feel your paws on the ground."

Flint followed Tina's lead, breathing in and out. He felt calmer and could see more clearly where he was. With the panic gone, the mist seemed to clear so Flint was able to find his way home.

As they reached Flint's burrow, he whispered, "Thank you Tina, for helping me find courage." Tina replied with a warm smile, "Remember, Flint, being brave doesn't mean not having fears. We all get scared sometimes. You're learning to be brave by facing your fears."

From that day on, Flint's family noticed a change in him. He faced his fears by using the deep breathing technique that Tina had taught him. He dared to explore a bit further away in the forest, feeling less timid each day, thanks to his newly found courage. Flint was very grateful for Tina's wise words.

* * *

Have you ever felt very scared by something new? How did you feel before and after?

Have you ever helped a friend who was scared? What did you do?

Build a Den (Pitch a Tent)

Put some sticks in the ground or lean them against a tree or a wall. Put a blanket over the sticks to make your den. Snuggle in with your toys or get a torch and a book to read. You could even pitch a tent in your garden. You can camp in your back garden.

Leaf Rubbing Collage

Collect leaves of various shapes and sizes. Place a leaf under a piece of paper and rub a crayon gently over it. You will see the leaf's veins and patterns. Use different leaves and different colour crayons. Then cut out the leaf rubbings and use them as body parts to make animals (ears, body, tail, legs, etc). Stick them on another paper to make a collage.

Moss Garden Terrarium

Moss likes shady spots. You won't need tools, just use your hands to gently peel a bit of moss (ask first). Clean it in water, then keep it in a sealed container for two days, removing any bugs.

For your moss garden, grab a jar and put rocks at the bottom for drainage, then add alittle bit of soil. Press in the moss, spray it with some water and watch it settle. Add sticks, figures or shells for a fun moss world.

Remember to spray with water from time to time to keep your moss garden growing.

Make a Sundial

A sundial is an ancient clock. A stick called *Gnomon* casts a shadow on a round plate with numbers. As the sun moves, the shadow moves too and falls on a number- the time of day.

Do you want to make your own? On a sunny day, stick a twig in the ground. Use small pebbles to mark where the shadow is at each hour. Set an alarm so you can do it throughout the day.

How many words can you make? Use the letters once only. Always include the letter in the middle of the wheel.

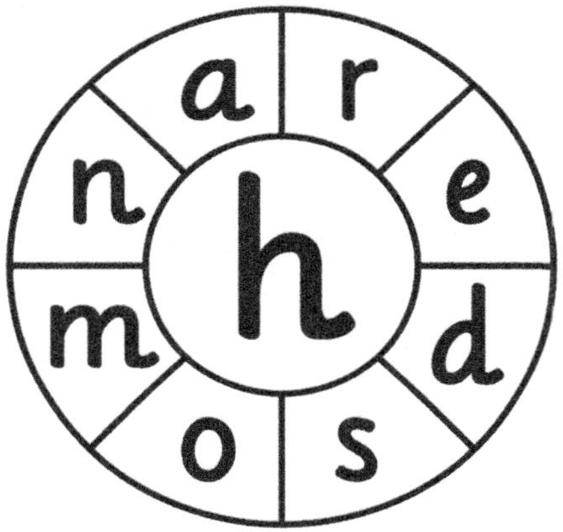

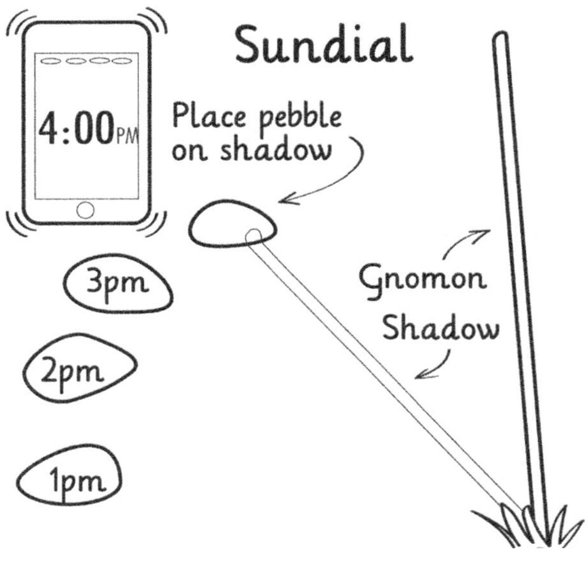

Tips for Parents

Help your child with learning about moss. There are lots of resources on the internet.

Have an alarm set for every hour and remind your child to place the next pebble on their sundial.

The Golden Acorn

There once were three best friends: Oliver, the wise owl; Sammy, the mischievous squirrel; and Benny, the hard-working beaver. They were renowned for their thrilling escapades and the special bond they shared.

One day, the friends caught wind of a legendary Golden Acorn: a magical nut said to have wish-granting powers. The trio embarked on an expedition to locate this enchanted treasure. Excitement brimmed in their hearts as they set out on their journey, facing challenges together, assisting each other in difficult situations and sealing their friendship with new memories.

After many days of exploration they stumbled upon the secluded glade where the Golden Acorn was rumoured to be. Lo and behold, there it was, radiating with a magical glow, perched atop a majestic oak tree! Oliver, the wise owl, soared gracefully and delicately plucked the Golden Acorn with his beak.

A magical voice resounded, "Congratulations! You each get one wish!"

Excitement filled the air! Sammy eagerly exclaimed, "I wish for an endless supply of the tastiest acorns!" Instantly, the glade was filled with delectable acorns, more than enough for Sammy.

Benny took a moment to ponder, then declared, "I wish for clean and pure water in our rivers so everyone in the forest can be happy and healthy." The air shimmered and a refreshing breeze swept through the glade.

Now it was Oliver's turn to speak. "My only wish is that I feel gratitude for all that I have."

The magical voice replied, "Very well, wise owl. Your choice shall be respected."

As the friends left the glade, Sammy and Benny revelled in the joy of their granted wishes: Sammy, with all the acorns he could ever desire and Benny witnessing the rivers sparkle with clean water. They laughed and played, sharing their satisfaction.

Time passed...

Sammy grew weary of eating only acorns and wished he'd asked for a variety of nuts not just acorns: to be honest he got a bit bored with them now. Benny, on the other hand, relished in the happiness that his wish for clean water had brought to the forest creatures. Oliver, who if you remember had no specific wish, found peace and contentment in the simple moments and the beauty of the forest.

And so the friends learned that happiness doesn't always come from getting what you want. Sometimes, the real magic lies in appreciating the journey, being content with what you have and sharing joy with others. As the three best friends continued their adventures, the forest flourished not just because of their magical wishes but with the wonder of true friendship, gratitude and finding beauty in every single thing.

Play In The Rain

Why does it sometimes rain a lot and other times just a little?

Rain Catcher

What containers would you use if you were in a competition to collect the most rainwater? Would you use a bucket or a plastic bottle?

Why not try it out with a few different containers and see for yourself?

Measure Rain

How would you design your own rain gauge? You could maybe use a clear plastic bottle or jar and secure a ruler to it.

What do you think would be the best spot to place your rain gauge to get accurate measurements?

Rain Music

Set up pots, pans, bowls or even tin foil outside – anything you think will sound nice when raindrops touch it. You could even place a xylophone out in the rain! What do you imagine the raindrops will sound like on these things? Give it a try. Explore nature's music!

Rain Art

Draw a rainbow or another pattern on watercolour paper. Place it flat in the rain and watch what happens. Don't leave it too long though or it will wash away. Then carefully pick up your rain art and hold it flat. Bring it inside and place it on some old towels to dry.

Make a Rainstick*

Randomly, hammer* in some nails along the length of a tube (such as a Pringles tube or a plastic bottle). The more nails, the better. Make sure one end is closed and add the fillers (pasta, rice, beans, beads, pebbles). Then close the other end and you are ready to start playing with your rainstick. Gently turn it over and listen to the sound it makes. You could look up South America on the map. This is where this instrument originated.

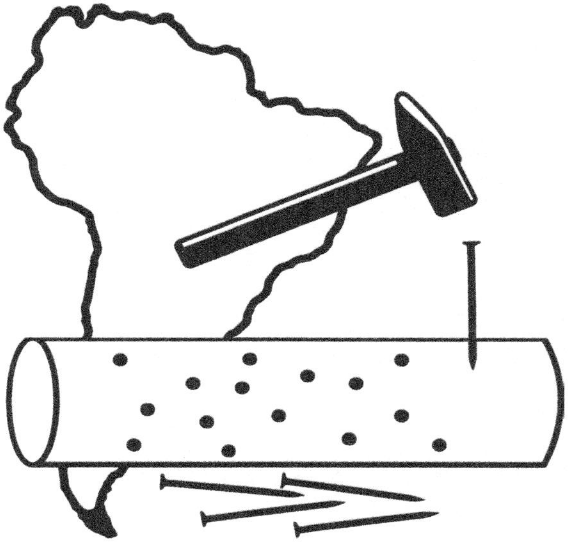

Tips for Parents

*Help your child with hammering the nails into the tube when making the rainstick. Take pictures of your child's creations and remind them to add their drawings to the Magic Moments to reMember.

Rusty's Hurdle Hop

In a hedge by a garden, lived a hare named Rusty,
Who dreamed of carrots and cabbages, oh so tasty.
A tall fence the hurdle, blocking his way,
No worries for Rusty, he knew how to play.

Found some crates nearby, not too far,
Stacked them up high, like reaching for a star.
Over the fence, with a jump so grand,
Into the garden, where veggies stand.

Carrots and cabbages, oh what a sight!
Rusty nibbled with pure delight.
Leaves so green, oh what a view!
Rusty munched, his happiness grew.

Moral of the story, simple and neat,
Be like Rusty, accept no defeat.
Be creative, do your best,
you'll find a solution to every test.

Challenge:

Learn to skip with a skipping rope.

Learn How To Solve Sudoku Puzzles

Fill the grid with the four shapes in such way that each shape is only used once in each row, in each column and in each box. (A box is marked as a 2 by 2 block.)

			△
	□		☆
☆		△	□
□	△		○

☆			□
△			○
	☆		
	△		

Fill the grid with the numbers 1, 2, 3, 4 in such way that each number is only used once in each row, in each column and in each box.

			2
2		3	1
	3		4

	2	3	4
3	4		1
	3		

Create Your Own Garden Sudoku

Create a garden-themed Sudoku puzzle with 4 different pictures (elements). You could choose flowers, vegetables, fruit or tools. Remember the one rule: each element must be only used once in each row, column and box.

P	M		
J	U	M	
		U	
U	J		

Tips for Parents

Help your child with developing logic.

Don't ever, ever, EVER guess! If you start guessing you will end up with doubles in your rows, columns and boxes. Think logically what is possible and especially what is not possible!

Little Wren's Big Dream

In a quiet corner of the old woods there lived a little wren called Jasper. Jasper was a small bird with brown and grey feathers. He loved singing happy songs that echoed through the trees.

Even though he was tiny, Jasper had a big dream: to make the best nest in the whole forest, strong and comfy. With his little wings, he worked hard collecting twigs, leaves and treasures from the forest floor. Other birds watched bewildered and the wise old owl hooted from his tree.

Days passed, and Jasper's nest began to take shape. His friends couldn't get it why he worked so hard.

Then, on a stormy day, the wind howled and raindrops tapped on the leaves. Many nests wobbled, some fell down but Jasper's nest stayed strong, just as he had built it. The other birds understood that Jasper's hard work had made his nest special. It made them think that maybe being patient and taking care when doing things could help them not just in building their nests but in other things too.

The wise old owl said, "Patience and care, my friends, patience and care... That's the secret to Jasper's extraordinary nest."

And so, whenever a young bird felt impatient, the older birds shared the story of Jasper, the little wren who patiently built a nest that stood strong in the storm. The young ones listened, learning the important lessons of patience and determination from Jasper's adventures.

The woods echoed with Jasper's happy song: a tune celebrating patience, hard work, and the joy of dreaming big. Jasper's story inspired every creature in the forest to follow their dreams with determination and resilience.

* * *

What big dreams do you have, like Jasper's dream of building the best nest?

How can you be patient and take care, just like Jasper, to make your dreams come true?

Bird Cafe

Did you know that you could use a pine cone, a spare apple or even cardboard to make bird feeders? Why not figure out how to do this by looking up some recipes online? The main ingredients are seeds and fat.

Don't use these: salted food, cooked food, peanuts, dried hard food, dried coconut, milk, mouldy food. They are very dangerous (poisonous) for birds.

Check out RSPB website for more suggestions on how to make your own bird feeders.

Birdwatching

Looking out your window, you might see birds in your garden or you can spot them at the park. Learning about birds is super fun! By identifying them, you can help protect them and their homes. With a special free guide from the RSPB website, you can learn about their needs and how to look after them. Plus, using binoculars lets you get a really close look! So, why not start your birdwatching adventure today and become a friend to feathered creatures everywhere?

				U ..-
A .-	F ..-.	K -.-	P .--.	V ...-
B -...	G --.	L .-..	Q --.-	W .--
C -.-.	H	M --	R .-.	X -..-
D -..	I ..	N -.	S ...	Y -.--
E .	J .---	O ---	T -	Z --..

Morse Code Bird Riddles

Q: What do you get if you cross a cat with a parrot ?

A: .- -.-. .- .-. .-. --- -

Q: What bird is always sad?

A: - .... . -... .-.. ..- . -... .. .-. -..

Q: What key won't open any door?

A: .- - ..- .-. -.- . -.--

Q: What kind of bird can carry the most weight?

A: - .... . -.-. .-. .- -. .

Q: What do you give a sick bird?

A: - .-- . . - -- . -. -

Secret Code

Make up a secret code to write and decode hidden messages. It's fun and helps you get better at spelling and thinking logically.

Tips for Parents

Help your child with making the bird feeders by supporting them in their online research.
Take pictures of your child's creations and remind them to add their drawings to the Magic Moments to reMember.

Honest Harvest

In a quiet part of Willowdale woods, Hilda the hedgehog tirelessly gathered apples for the winter. Every day she carefully stacked a small pile beneath a tree, went home to rest and carried them home the next day.

One day, returning to her spot, Hilda found her pile had mysteriously disappeared. Confused, she gathered another pile and went back home exhausted.

However, the following day the treasure stash was gone again and this made Hilda very upset!

Determined to figure out what was going on, she gathered a third pile of apples but this time she didn't go home. She snuggled nearby to rest.

In a quiet part of Willowdale woods, two young hedgehog brothers, Harry and Harvey, stumbled upon a small pile of apples, nicely stacked under a tree. Hungry and not thinking too much about it, they enjoyed the unexpected feast. What delicious apples they were!

To the brothers' delight, a new pile appeared the next day, and they happily devoured it again, thinking they were incredibly fortunate.

However, on the third day, when another pile materialised, Harry and Harvey exchanged puzzled glances. Something seemed off about the magical appearance of apple piles, day after day.

While Hilda rested nearby, keeping watch on her carefully stacked pile of apples, Harry and Harvey approached. As they scanned the surroundings, their eyes fell upon Hilda who was resting under the tree.

A cheerful comment escaped Harry's lips, "Hi, Hilda! Fair play to you! You found the pile of apples before us today!" but Harvey nudged his brother to be quiet. A realisation swept over the hedgehogs: the apples they had enjoyed might not have been meant for them... "Was it you who gathered these apples, Hilda? And all the others before?" a pang of guilt was in Harvey's voice. The two brothers had to tell the truth and they apologised to Hilda, "We're really sorry for taking without asking."

Hilda smiled and responded kindly, "Integrity is doing the right thing even when no one is watching. I accept your apology. Now let's work together to gather more apples and we will share them properly this time."

Puppet Play

First, gather some puppets. You can either use ones you have or make your own with socks or paper bags. Then, it's story time! Create a simple story using your puppets. You can use your imagination or act out a story you love. Next, find a spot to set up your puppet theatre. This could be a table, behind a sofa, or even a cardboard box with a hole for the stage. Once you're all set up, it's time to bring your characters to life! Move your puppets and speak for them. Have good creative fun!

In the Matchbox...

This challenge is all about being super observant and spotting those teeny wonders in nature. Grab a matchbox and go outside on a mission: See how many tiny treasures you can squeeze in your matchbox. But guess what? When that matchbox is full, your collecting adventure is done! So, be picky with what you pick!

Nature Scavenger Hunt

Make a list of things you want to find. Then grab your list and go searching. When you find one of the things on your list, check it off and maybe draw a picture to remember where you found it or what it looked like. This is a game to see who can find all the treasures first.

Apples in Boxes

There are three boxes: a brown one, a red one and a white one. They are holding a total of ten apples.
The brown box has *one more* apple than the red box.
The red box has *three fewer* apples than the white box.

How many apples are in each box?

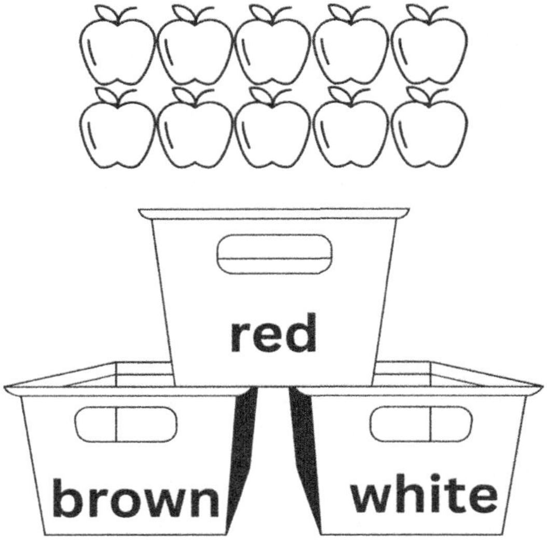

TIP: Get 10 objects to represent the apples and 3 cups to represent the boxes. Then play around moving the objects in the cups.

Tips for Parents

Be good attentive audience for the puppet show.
Explain the meaning of "fewer" as your child may not understand it.
Take pictures of your child's creations and remind them to add their drawings to the Magic Moments to reMember.

Beneath the Blooms

In a serene nook of the garden, two sunflower seeds, Sunny and Luna, lay nestled in the nurturing soil. Sunny sprouted eagerly, reaching for the sun, while Luna's growth was slower, her roots venturing deep into the earth.

Sunny burst forth, boasting vibrant petals that drew everyone's attention. "Look at me!" she'd proudly exclaim, revelling in the spotlight. Meanwhile, Luna's growth was subtle, her buds closed, quietly tuning into the hidden murmurs of the earth and learning from Mycella, the ruler of the underground.

Observing Luna's focus on the soil, Sunny often joked, "In the dirt again, Luna? No wonder you'll never look pretty."

As Sunny's flamboyant beauty captured the garden's gaze, Luna continued her quiet absorption of the earth's silent language. Then, as Sunny's once-vibrant petals began to droop and her stem weakened, Luna's own transformation began. Her closed buds gradually unfolded into a magnificent array of colours, drawing the garden's attention.

Confused by her own fading beauty, Sunny turned to Luna, "How are you becoming so beautiful all of a sudden?" she asked, a mix of surprise, annoyance and curiosity in her voice.

Luna rustled her leaves softly and hinted at her connection to the earth's whispers and the teachings from Mycella. "There's more below the surface than meets the eye, Sunny," she replied mysteriously.

As Luna shared her knowledge, the significance of the underground world and the guidance of Mycella slowly unfolded. Sunny learned about mycelium, this invisible yet vital network that sustains life.

"So, it's not just dirt?" Sunny pondered Luna's transformation. Sunny realised how she got distracted and she missed something important- connecting to the earth's endless source of energy and wisdom. Sunny understood that uniting with mycelium might hold the key to rejuvenating her fading beauty.

* * *

Can you think of something that's important for you even if it's not easy to see?

Can you think of something that took time (like Luna's growth) but turned out really nice?

"How Plants Drink" Experiment

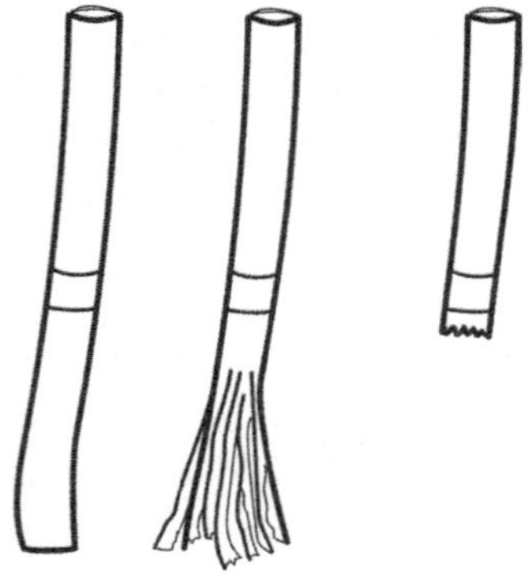

Gather the following materials:

> pebbles, marbles or rice ("soil")
> kitchen roll paper towels ("plants"),
> 3 plastic cups ("planting pots"),
> food colouring ("plant food"),
> tape, water, scissors

Roll three paper towels and tape the middle so they keep their shape.
Let's call the part under the tape "the roots" and let's call the part above the tape "the stem".

Keep one paper roll as it is. Let's imagine this is a plant with a TAP ROOT.
Cut the "root" side of the second paper roll into strips. This represents a plant with FIBROUS ROOTS.
Cut the third paper roll off under the tape. Let's call it STEM WITH NO ROOTS.

Place TAP ROOT and FIBROUS ROOTS in a cup ("planting pot") and then fill the cup with "soil" pressing around the "roots". Fill a third cup with "soil" and press STEM WITH NO ROOTS slightly into the "soil".

Pour coloured water "plant food" into the "soil" of the three cups and observe how it travels up the "stems" of TAP ROOT and FIBROUS ROOTS. Then give each "plant" a little push, pretending you are the wind.

What do you notice?
What does it mean?

STEM WITH NO ROOTS *falls* over easily and doesn't absorb much water.

Root Mapping

Carefully pull out some plants/weeds with their roots. Shake off as much of the soil as possible and then place on a big newspaper. Observe the roots with a magnifying glass and discuss your discoveries.

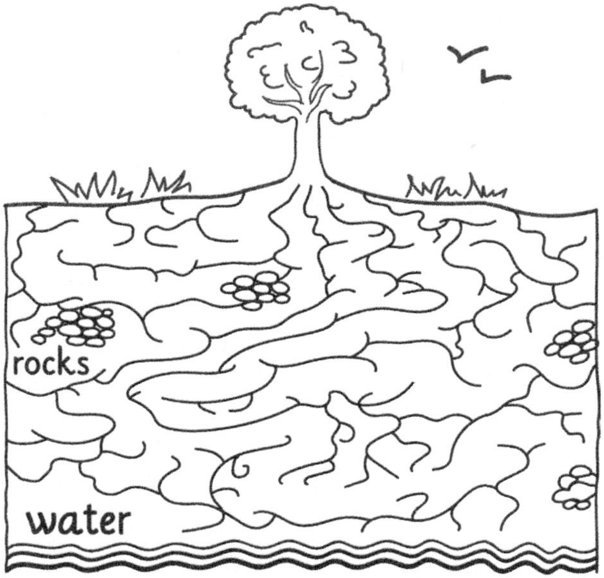

Pressed Flowers

Choose some beautiful flowers. Get some baking paper, fold it in half and put the flowers inside it, like a sandwich. Place the flower sandwich between the pages of a book. The baking paper will keep the flowers from staining or sticking to the pages. Close the book tightly and stack heavy books on top to press the flowers flat. Leave them like that for a few days until they are completely dry. Once dry, the flowers will be flat and ready to use for making colourful cards, bookmarks or pretty pictures.

Tips for Parents

Some flowered are thicker and take longer to dry out. To avoid the flowers staining the book pages, fold a piece of paper and place the flowers between the two sides, then put inside the book. Take pictures of the experiment.

Meet Mycella, the Soil Queen

I live deep beneath the soil, where it's dark and snug. I'm Mycella, the Underground Queen, but people also call me Mycelium.

I can't see or hear: I have no eyes or ears; but I sense the earth's vibes and know when I am needed. My home is everywhere in the ground. I gracefully glide and weave through the soil. Together with the roots of plants we have our secret club beneath your feet.

As my delicate threads explore the soil, I can sense if a plant friend is in distress. "Mycella, help! I'm thirsty but the soil is dry!" Straight away, my threads reach out like straws, sipping water and sending it to the plant. The leaves perk up and the plant cheers up, "Thanks, Mycella! You're our queen, our underground hero."

I enjoy making friends with different plants and helping them to stay in touch. I even make special connections possible, joining mother trees with their baby saplings underground.

But my royal duties extend beyond social affairs. I am a dedicated chef as well. When I come across a pile of old leaves, I diligently break them up into nutritious pieces and turn them into a delicious soup for the plants. Though I lack a mouth, I ensure everyone enjoys a nourishing meal.

Apart from being a water provider, a skilful chef and a matchmaker, I deal with dangerous tasks too. When I sense the worried whispers of my friends, "There is an oil spill! It's making us ill!" I cannot turn away. My threads stretch and I clean up the mess which is usually caused by humans. This is a challenging job but it is super important. The soil expresses its gratitude and the plants above ground breathe a sigh of relief.

Sometimes, when the conditions are right, I burst out with joy and beautiful mushrooms emerge! They are my messengers, coming out in different shapes and colours, revealing to the world the secret that I'm around. The mushrooms burst forth carrying my tiny spores.

Even though you can't see me, I am here. It is because of me that the old becomes new and the natural world remains a happy place.

* * *

Think about Mycella's role as the "underground hero.' Can you recall a time when you felt like a hero, helping someone or something that needed support? What happened?

Mushroom Spore Prints

Only use edible mushrooms from the shop. Choose flat, open ones. Don't pick mushrooms in the wild because they may be poisonous.

1. Trim the mushroom and remove the stem. Mushrooms are delicate so be very gentle.

2. Place the cap of the mushroom face down on card or paper (gills facing down).

3. Place a bowl over the mushroom. This will make the mushroom release its spores. They will drop from the gills and form patterns on the paper below.

4. Leave the mushroom under the bowl for about 12-24 hours.

5. Remove the bowl and gently lift up the mushroom to reveal the prints!

Spores are very, very tiny. New mushrooms grow from them.

It's like opening a present: you don't know what you are going to get. Show your friends!

The prints are made from the spores of the mushroom. If you rub the prints with your fingers, they will smudge. You could ask an adult to spray them with a fixative spray.

Paper Mache Earth

Dip newspaper strips into paper mache paste and stick them over a balloon to make the round shape of the globe. When it dries, paint the continents and oceans and think about the fantastic mycelium connecting the plants underground. Isn't that awesome?!

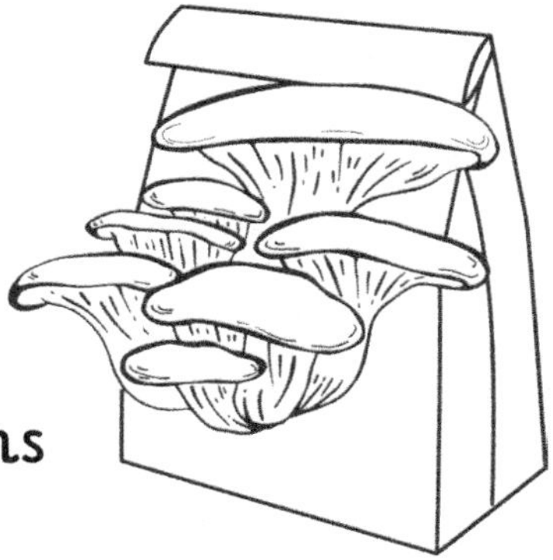

Grow Mushrooms at Home

Ask your adults to buy you a mushroom growing kit. There are some affordable ones. This way you can see how mushrooms grow. You will learn about the amazing mycelium and you'll harvest some tasty mushrooms that you grew yourself!

Tips for Parents

Help your child choose mushrooms for their art from the shop and help with spraying the spore print with a fixative. Take pictures of your child's creations and remind them to add their drawings to the Magic Moments to reMember.

Encourage your child to use their imagination and create stories of their own. They could draw pictures to go with the stories - there is space for both their writing and their drawings in this chapter.

Chapter 8 - My Stories
Create
Make-believe
Imagination
Imagination
Daydream
Pretend
8

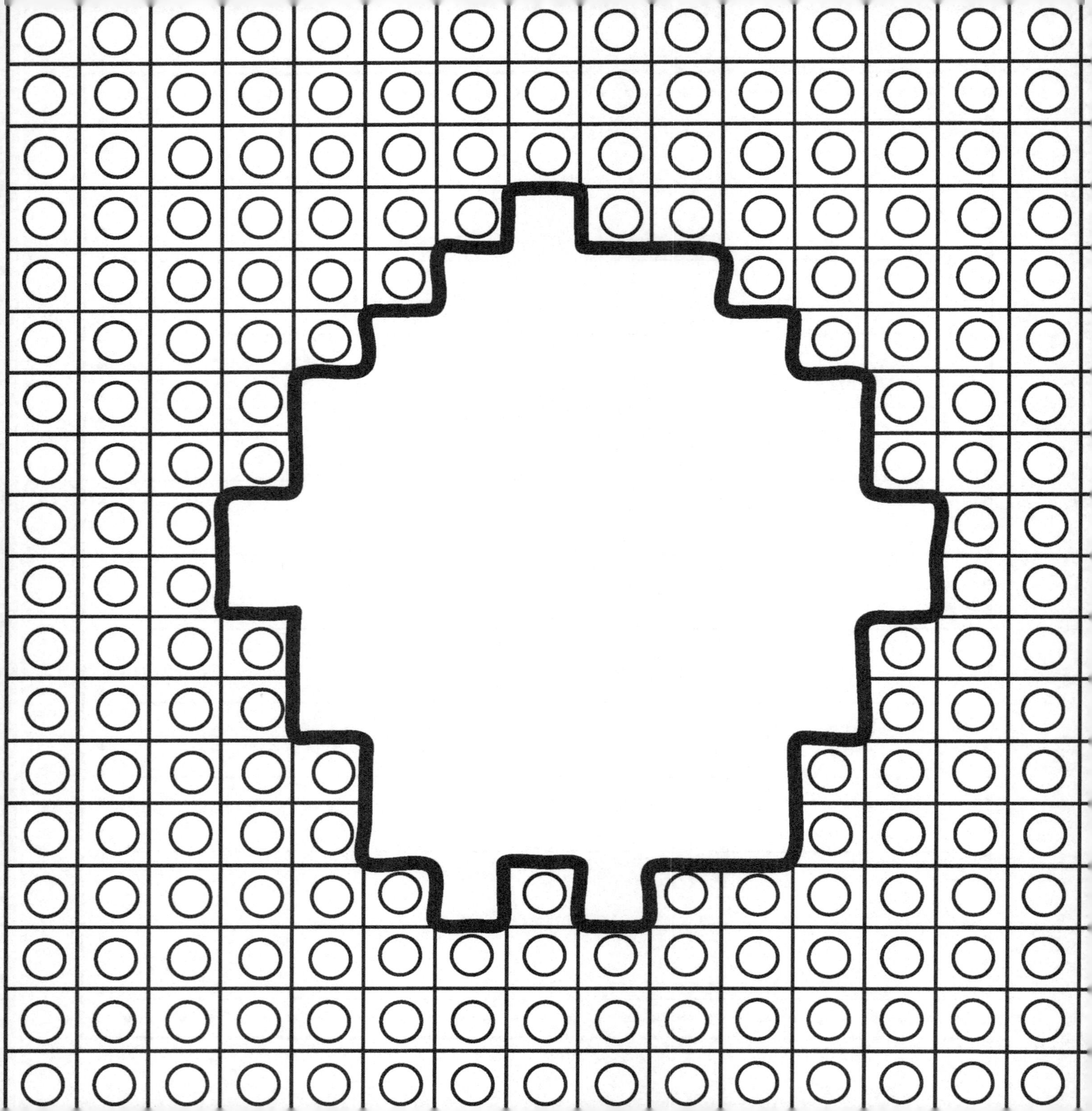

Your first crop to harvest would probably be lettuce, followed by strawberries and peas. At this point it will be a great idea to teach your child how to use the kitchen scales so they can record the weight of the fruit and vegetables they pick from their garden.

Teach your child how to tell if the plants are ready to be harvested, how to pick the food they have grown and then let them be responsible for their own harvest. Remind your young gardener to weigh the produce before cooking or eating it and to record each harvest in this chapter, “Harvest Time”.

At the end of the growing season, you could offer to help your child add up the weight of all the produce so they can see the total amount of food they have grown. This could be a great life lesson in confidence-boosting, appreciation and gratitude.

Tasty, yummy food !
I grew it myself !
SALAD
Chapter 9 - Harvest Time

9

Harvest Time

Weeks passed.

Sam and Mia's Gardening Book was filling up with notes.

But something was happening with the potatoes.

Mr Parker, our potatoes look ill...
What have we done wrong?

It's all good, kiddos. The leaves are dying off to let the potatoes in the soil fatten up. For this variety we count 16 weeks from planting before we can dig them out.

Sam leafed through the pages of his Book.

"We planted them on 29th of March, Mr Parker!
Let me count the weeks. 1, 2, 3..." Sam began.

"Two more weeks to go. Not long left, Mia!"

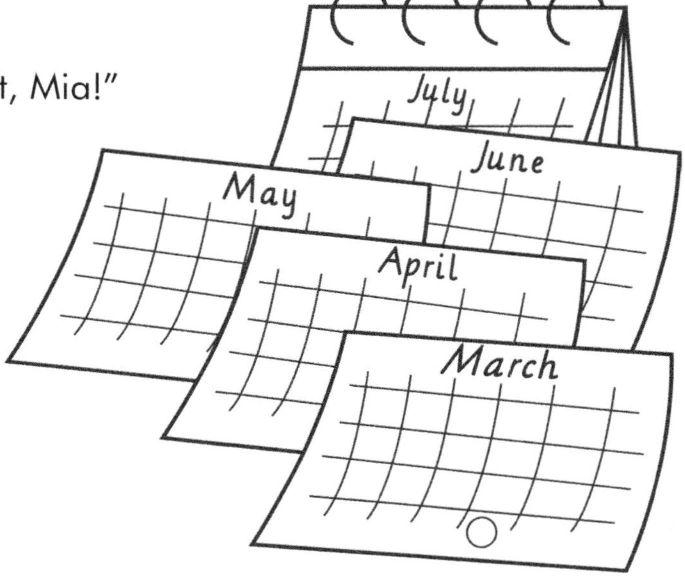

Two weeks later, the twins and their parents dug out the potatoes.

Sam's grow bag had 24 potatoes in it

and Mia was super happy with her 26!

Mum, Dad, we want to do it again!
Can we have two more grow bags please!

My Harvest Log

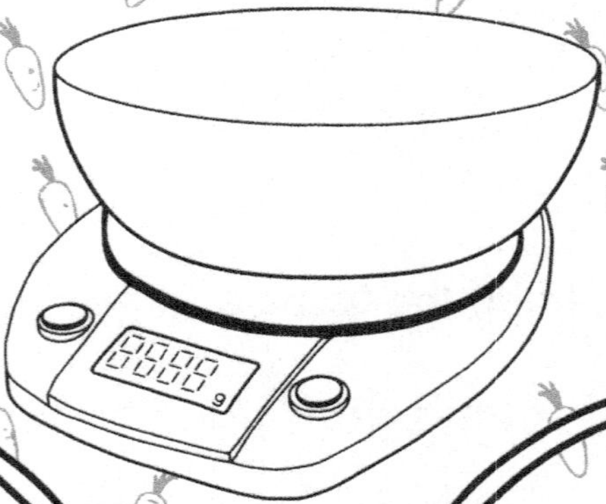

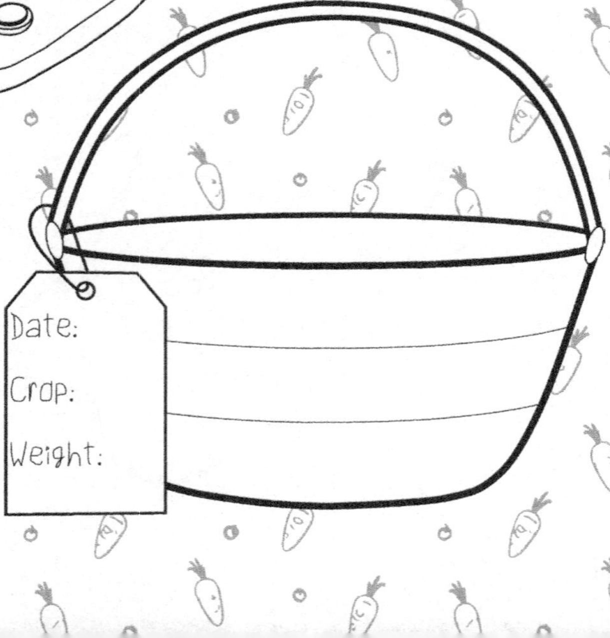

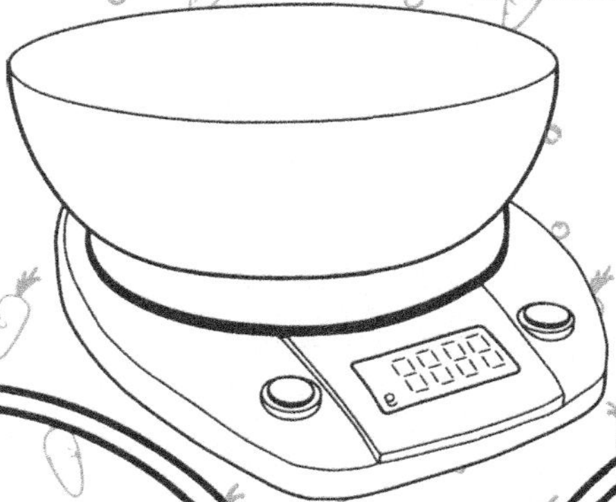

Remember to weigh your harvest!

My Harvest Log

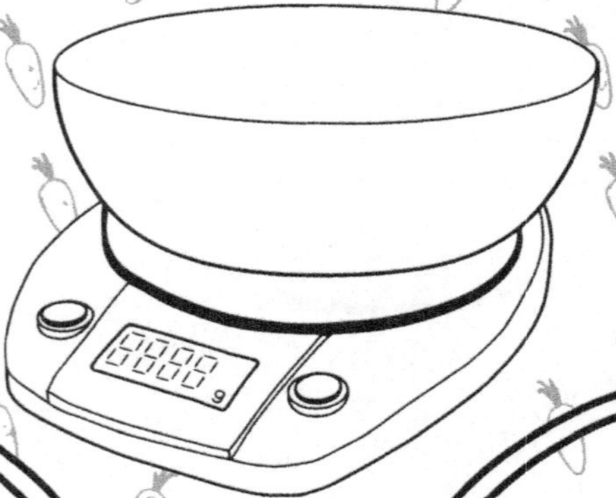

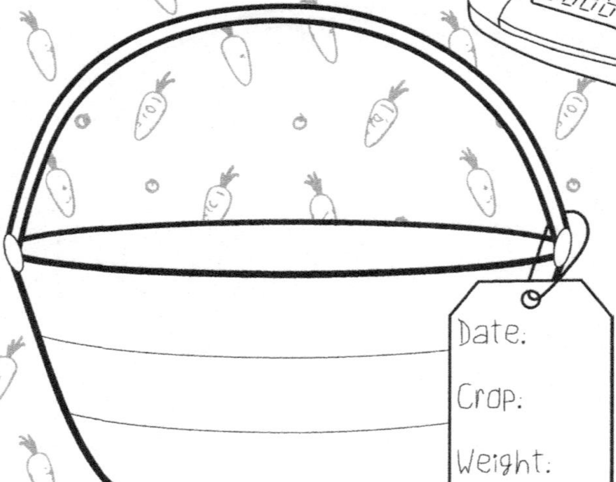

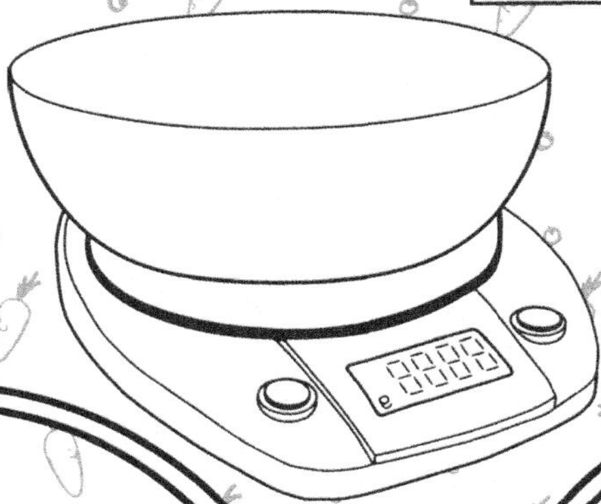

Remember to weigh your harvest!

My Harvest Log

Date:
Crop:
Weight:
Date:
Crop:
Weight:
Remember to weigh your harvest!
Date:
Crop:
Weight:
Date:
Crop:
Weight:

My Harvest Log

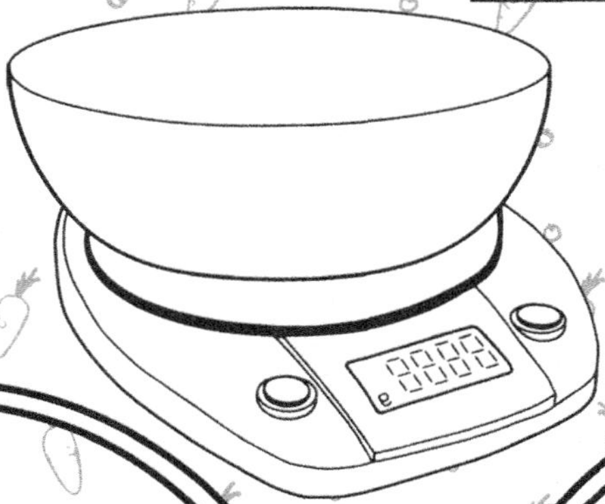

Remember to weigh your harvest!

My Harvest Log

Date:
Crop:
Weight:
Date:
Crop:
Weight:
Remember to weigh your harvest!
Date:
Crop:
Weight:
Date:
Crop:
Weight:

My Harvest Log

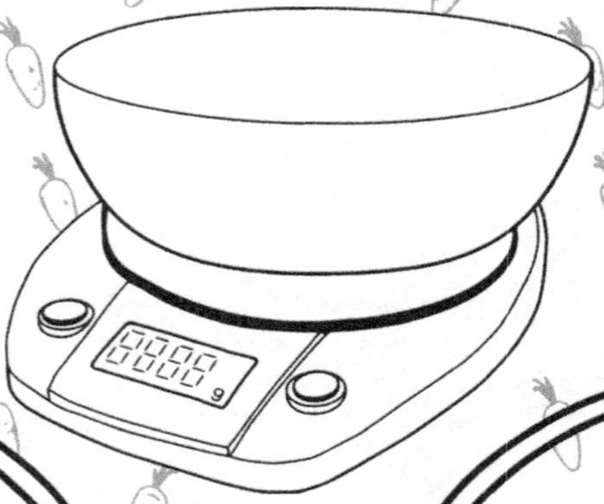

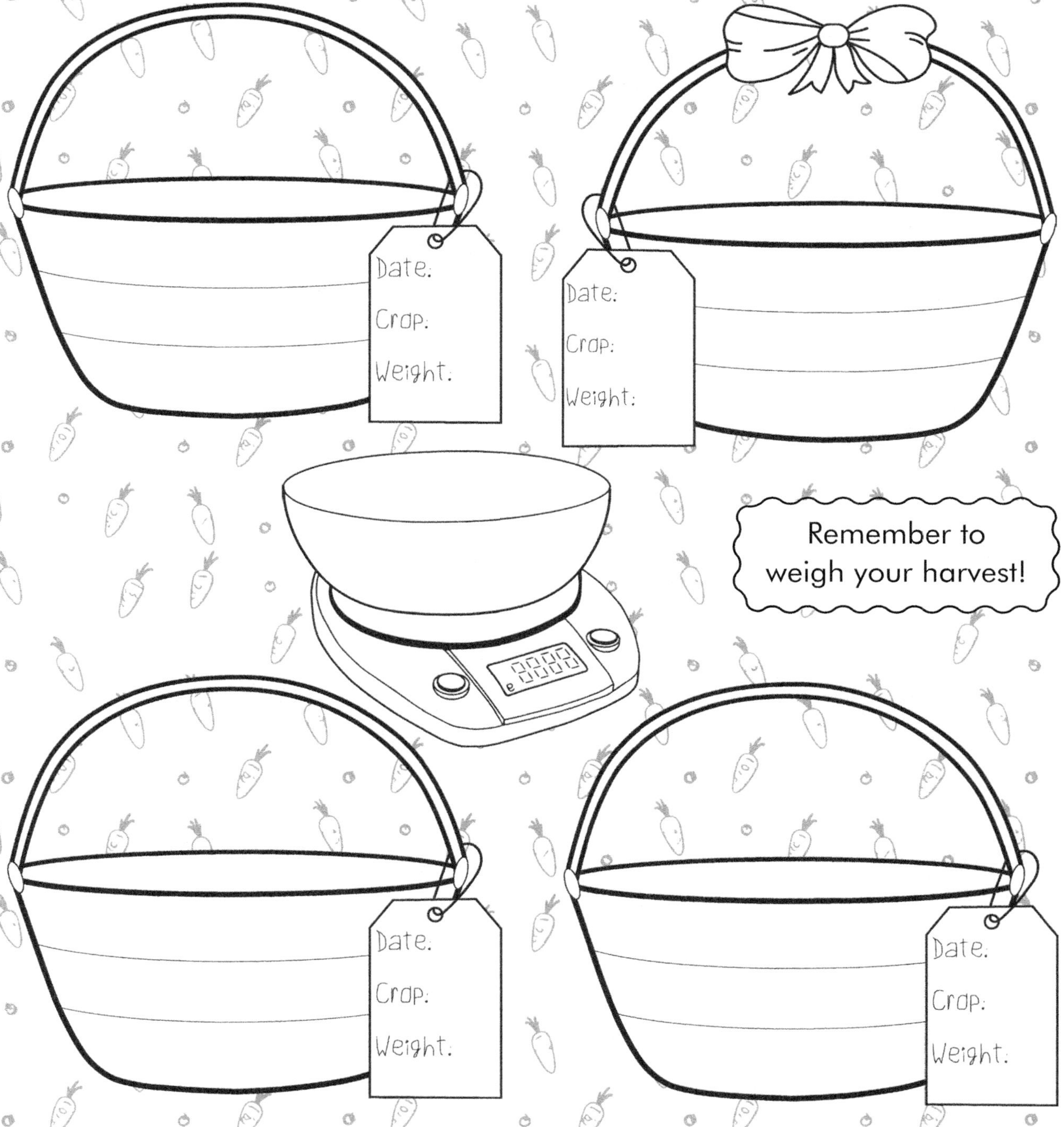
Date:
Crop:
Weight:
Date:
Crop:
Weight:
Remember to weigh your harvest!
Date:
Crop:
Weight:
Date:
Crop:
Weight:

My Harvest Log

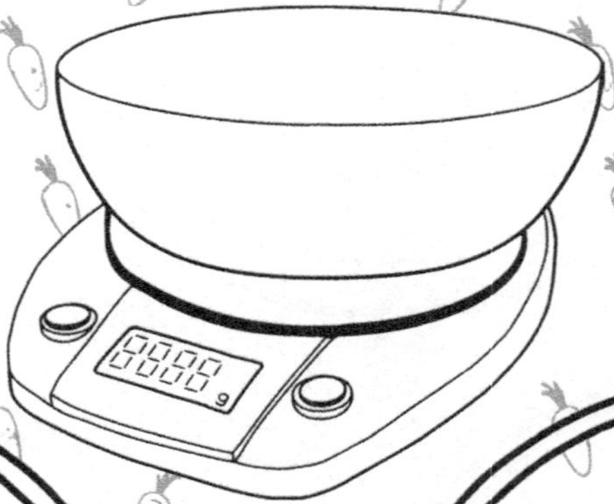

Date:
Crop:
Weight:
Date:
Crop:
Weight:
Remember to weigh your harvest!
Date:
Crop:
Weight:
Date:
Crop:
Weight:

My Harvest Log

Date:
Crop:
Weight:
Date:
Crop:
Weight:
Remember to weigh your harvest!
Date:
Crop:
Weight:
Date:
Crop:
Weight:

My Harvest Log
Date:
Crop:
Weight:
Date:
Crop:
Weight:
0000 g
Date:
Crop:
Weight:
Date:
Crop:
Weight:

Date:
Crop:
Weight:
Date:
Crop:
Weight:
Remember to weigh your harvest!
Date:
Crop:
Weight:
Date:
Crop:
Weight:

In "Garden Cooking" you can find practical recipes for the fresh produce your young gardener has lovingly grown. It's a simple guide to making the most of the harvest. Encourage your child to participate in the kitchen, practicing cutting skills on easy-to-cut vegetables. For tougher ones like pumpkin, carrot and beetroot, they can observe and help.

Please note, the recipes are rough guidelines and simple suggestions without exact measurements, allowing room for creativity and flexibility in the kitchen.

10

Wash the lettuce. Cut the tomato & cucumber. Grate the carrot & beetroot. Mix together in a bowl. Dressing: olive oil, a pinch of sugar, a pinch of salt, lemon juice and (if you like it) some garlic.

Cut up the pumpkin. Remove the seeds. Place the pumpkin chunks (skin down) onto a roasting tray and put in the oven for 20min. Turn them over and roast for 20min more. When they cool down take off the skin (optional) and enjoy!

Mix a little olive oil with a couple of teaspoons of paprika. Wash well and cut into wedges a few of your lovely potatoes. Mix the potatoes with the oil/paprika and then lay them on a baking tray with tin foil. Bake at 220C for 40min, turning them over after 20min. Yummy!

Runner Beans Snack

Cut off the top tail of the runner beans. Cut the beans in 4-5cm long pieces. Heat a little oil in a pan. Pop in some crushed garlic. Fry for a couple of minutes. Add the runner beans and some little soy sauce. Sprinkle a pinch of sugar and black pepper to taste.

Thick Pea Soup

Put the peas in a saucepan and fry with a little garlic and butter. Cover with water and some salt. Simmer for 20min. Dust with cornflour a little at a time stirring continuously until thickened. Add salt and some sugar to taste.

Strawberries & Cream

Exactly that!
Or you could swap the cream for yogurt.

About the Authors

Meet Desi Stefanova, a primary school teacher for twenty years who focussed on the 6-8 age group. During these years of interaction with young minds Desi acquired a profound understanding of how children learn. Transitioning from teaching to gardening, Desi, together with Chris, transformed a simple patch of land into a productive source of homegrown food. Drawing from these hands-on experiences, not only did Desi cultivate this organic haven but also authored a thoughtful gardening guide for adults. Her green fingers are deeply rooted in childhood memories, happily spent alongside her dad, discovering gardener's secrets. Growing up, her mum's encouragement in exploring a wide range of activities created the foundation for curiosity, love for learning and a variety of interests. Now, channelling her diverse skills and prior professional experience, Desi has created this engaging and heart-warming gardening journal for children and carers alike. This book is centred around growing fruit and vegetables in pots at home but it also teaches reading, writing, maths, problem solving and various life skills to enrich school curriculum and nurture family connections..

Enter Chris Ogle, a computer software engineer and business owner by trade (plus a self-trained carpenter), boasting decades of experience and a unique talent for foreseeing trends. Shifting from the fast-paced tech world to the tranquillity of gardening, invited by the simple request "Would you help if I got an allotment?", Chris didn't just plant seeds, but sowed the concept for a deeper connection to nature and use of his latent woodworking skills. His childhood memories of an array of fresh vegetables grown in the family garden by his dad and cooked to perfection by a doting mum came in handy. Recognizing the alarming societal disconnection from nature and its repercussions on health, Chris envisioned more than just a garden — he foresaw a tool to encourage families to get enthusiastic about growing food again. This book, born from his visionary spark, aims to teach children essential skills, not just in growing food but in rediscovering the simple joys of nature.

Together, Chris and Desi seamlessly weave their diverse expertise and shared passion into the fabric of this enchanting children's gardening journal.

Disclaimer

"My First Gardening Book" features activities that may pose potential health risks. Please note that any reader or individuals under their supervision participating in these activities do so at their own risk. The authors and the publisher disclaim any legal responsibility for harm, injury, damage, loss or legal consequences resulting from the use or misuse of the activities, crafts, tools and suggestions presented in this book.

By organising any activity from this book, you affirm that you are fully informed about allergies, health conditions and all associated risks for participants. You accept responsibility for those involved, understanding that the authors bear no liability for any activity-related incidents.

Parents and guardians are urged to exercise utmost caution and closely supervise young children using sharp items like garden and craft tools, scissors, knives, etc.

Additionally, please note that it is illegal to carry out any activities from this book on private land without the owner's permission. It is crucial to obey laws related to the protection of land, property and animals.

Further Support

If you have further questions, need support or if you want to hang out with like-minded people, we provide assistance and a friendly community in our Discord Server called ***Garden Growers.*** You can join it for free by scanning this QR code:

Printed in Great Britain
by Amazon

46125972R00143